Driving Scenic New Zealand

A GUIDE TO TOURING NEW ZEALAND BY ROAD

DAVE CHOWDHURY

GINZ™.com

Hi Guys
Hope you have a
great time in New Zealand

Operated by Michael Nees Travel NZ Ltd
PO Box 4436, Christchurch
New Zealand

Email: info@ginz.com
Internet: http://www.ginz.com
Phone: 64 3 366 4486   Fax: 64 3 366 4452

kind Regards
Jane ☺

Dave Chowdhury is a Wellington writer and editor. In 2000 he completed a degree in international relations and political philosophy, then took the first job that came along – writing this guide. Despite assertions to the contrary, his friends remain unconvinced that spending summer travelling New Zealand constituted work.

ACKNOWLEDGEMENTS

I would like to acknowledge all at Craig Potton Publishing, especially Betzy Iannuzzi, Robbie Burton, Craig Potton, Noleen Campbell, Tina Delceg and Phillippa Duffy; and those friends and family who provided fine company and floor space in the course of my travels: Roy and Eileen Chowdhury, Kevin and Margaret O'Connor, Don and Margaret Lamont, Alison Ballance, Brendan Kane, Terry Sumner, Manfred Meyer, Irene Cahill and Gunnar Kaschka, Fred Holmes and Fi Acheson, Katherine Curran and Warren of Surat Bay Lodge, John Skilton and Suzy Ruddenklau, the Mathias Family, Steve Davies, Pat and Cheryl Sole, Marie Taylor and Richard Croad, Rob Kirkwood and Paula Marshall, John Hilhorst and Cath Gilmour, Ray and Christine Bellringer. A special thanks must go to Naomi O'Connor, my occasional assistant researcher, notetaker and coffee consultant, who made me stop at places I might otherwise have ignored.

Text: Dave Chowdhury

Production: Tina Delceg, Phillippa Duffy, Robbie Burton

Maps: Base maps supplied by Terralink Ltd; additional map work by Tina Delceg

Photography: Craig Potton

Cover Design: Jo Williams

Cover Photo: Road to Aoraki/Mt Cook by Ben Simmons

Printing: Astra Print Ltd, Wellington, NZ

Published by: Craig Potton Publishing
98 Vickerman Street, PO Box 555, Nelson, New Zealand
www.craigpotton.co.nz

CONTENTS

Introduction	4
North Island Route Key	8
North Island Map	9
North Island Routes	10-75
South Island Route Key	76
South Island Map	77
South Island Routes	78-141
Index	142

Cape Reinga

About this guide

When I was a kid growing up in the 1960s and 70s our family would load up the car – a modest Cortina in the early years, and later the ubiquitous Antipodean Holden – for long summer holidays. Being recent immigrants from the UK and India, exploring our new home gave these holidays an added impetus. New Zealand isn't that big a place and the web of roads that criss-crossed the countryside gave us access to faraway places in relatively short order. These holidays took us from our home in Taranaki to Auckland and the Far North, Rotorua, Taupo, Hawke's Bay, Wellington, and occasionally to the South Island.

Back then roads weren't as good as they are now. I remember the terrible dusty unsealed winding roads between Napier and Taupo, through the Manawatu Gorge and in the Far North. Even some of the sealed routes were tortuous winding affairs through the North Island hinterland.

Since then, most of these roads have been sealed, straightened and no doubt made safer. The web of roads remains, the major difference is that there are more cars on the road than ever. That and the fact that tourism has become a major world industry, which has led to the development of a greatly expanded tourism infrastructure in New Zealand.

The other significant shift has been from the pre-arranged package tour of New Zealand to 'free and independent travel' holidays. Instead of plying the traditional tourist trade routes by bus, train or plane, tourists are travelling everywhere in hired campervans and rental vehicles, or increasingly, buying a car for the duration of their holiday, camping or staying in the many backpackers and homestays that have sprung up around the country.

This new guide is a response to this trend in tourism. In it you will find descriptions of the major touring routes in New Zealand. Highlighted are the major places of interest, tourist facilities, travel times and distances, interesting side trips, walks, campgrounds, places where you might find a good coffee or a bite to eat. I won't claim it as being an exhaustive guide, more a greatest hits if you like. What this book is not is a guide to major destinations or accommodation – instead it is about the places and landscapes that lie in-between, to be used in conjunction with your Lonely Planet, Rough Guide or AA accommodation book.

Driving in New Zealand

- **Driver licences**
  All drivers must have a current and/or an international driver licence. Vehicles are right-hand drive, and must be driven on the left-hand side of the road.

- **Safety belts**
  Wearing safety belts is compulsory for all occupants of a vehicle. Children under 5 must be restrained with an approved children's car restraint.

- **Speed limits**
  Speed limits in New Zealand are 100 km/h on the open road, and 50 km/h in built-up areas. LSZ (Limited

Speed Zones) means you must drive 50 km/h in adverse conditions (for instance poor weather) otherwise the 100 km/h limit applies. A range of limits applies at road works (30–50 km/h) and on the outskirts of urban areas (usually 70 km/h). If you're towing a trailer the limit is 80 km/h, likewise if driving a bus or truck it's 80 km/h.

■ **Intersections**
- Always use your indicators when turning (give 3 seconds warning before beginning the turn).
- Give way to all traffic not turning.
- Give way to all traffic crossing or approaching from your right.

■ **Roundabouts**
- Always turn left into a roundabout.
- Give way to all traffic on your right.
- Indicate when you are about to leave the intersection.

■ **Traffic Lights**
North American drivers are advised that there is no free left turn on a red traffic light.

■ **Rental vehicles**
Tourists over 21 years with an appropriate licence can rent virtually any type of vehicle in New Zealand – from large campervans and all terrain four-wheel-drives to small two-door hatchbacks. Prices are variable and you tend to get what you pay for. Thus at the cheaper end of the range (between $30–$40 a day, unlimited mileage) you're likely to get a vehicle which is underpowered (1500 cc or less) and unlikely to have a good or functioning stereo system – considerations if you're planning a long trip and if there's more than two of you. Choose a rental company that offers Automobile Association breakdown assistance. Hirers are responsible for maintaining oil and water levels, but if your vehicle burns oil, keep the receipts and ask to be reimbursed as it's the company's responsibility to provide you with a well-maintained vehicle. Insurance cover is usually provided, but can involve some hefty excesses ($750–$1500). Insurance won't cover broken windscreens in some cases. There are also insurance issues around unsealed roads – see next section.

■ **Unsealed roads**
Some routes described in this book have sections of unsealed road. For the most part these roads are well-graded and maintained, and present few difficulties when driven cautiously. New Zealanders drive these roads confidently, sometimes too confidently. But for the overseas tourists used to paved highways, gravel roads can present a serious hazard.

In one accident I came across while researching this book, two German tourists put their car 50 m down a bank above Lake Waikaremoana, having braked too hard on a corner and skidded off the road. Their vehicle stopped just metres above the water – they were extremely lucky. Unfortunately accidents involving tourists on gravel roads are commonplace, particularly on popular drives like the Catlins coast section of the Southern Scenic Route in Southland.

The best advice is to drive unsealed roads slowly – you're on holiday after all! Driving slowly gives you more control and allows a greater margin for reacting to other more confident drivers and irresponsible local drivers travelling too fast for the conditions. If you're driving an automatic, always select second or low gear to give yourself a measure of control on corners, and lessening your reliance on braking.

Secondly, if you're in a rental vehicle, check the fine print of your rental agreement because some don't insure drivers on an unsealed road, while others exclude particular roads such as any road north of Coromandel township, the last few kilometres to Cape Reinga, any mountain or skifield access road, the Skippers Gorge near Queenstown. The rental company argument that unsealed roads would be sealed if they were popular is misplaced when it comes to, for example, the last few kilometres of SH 1 to Cape Reinga. If this is an issue, renegotiate the insurance agreement, or find another rental company.

- **Slow drivers**

  I thoroughly recommend slow driving, but having said that, slow drivers on New Zealand roads are a particular source of frustration for following motorists, especially on hilly or winding terrain where overtaking opportunities are limited. Campervan drivers need to be aware of this. Convenient as these vehicles are, they are also slow, cumbersome and belch smelly diesel fumes, which is annoying to anyone behind. The simple rule for the sightseeing driver is pull over at every opportunity to let others pass – it's such an easy and courteous thing to do.

- **Fuel**

  Petrol and diesel are widely available, but prices vary, wildly in some cases, the further you get away from main centres or routes, or when OPEC alters production, in which case rapid falls and rises in price come with little warning. In some areas the price of fuel amounts to daylight robbery, particularly in the

Maori words commonly used in place names

awa – river or valley	niwa – rainbow	roa – long
hua – plenty	nui – big	roto – lake
ika – fish	pa – fortified village	rua – two
inanga – whitebait	pari – cliff	tahuna – sand dunes, beach
iti – small	pounamu – greenstone	tapu – sacred or forbidden
kai – food	puke – hill	wai – water
manga – stream or tributary	rae – cape	whanga – bay or inlet
maunga – mountain	rangi – sky	whare – house
moana – sea	repo – swamp	whenua – land or country
motu – island	rere – waterfall	

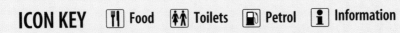

ICON KEY 🍴 Food 🚻 Toilets ⛽ Petrol ℹ️ Information

Far North and the South Island West Coast. My advice is to fill up at the major towns and cities where fuel is usually cheaper than the smaller localities in-between.

Visitor Information Centres, toilets, cafés

One of the greatest improvements for tourists and New Zealand travellers has been the establishment of an excellent network of visitor information centres. These will be found at all major centres and tourist destinations, usually well signposted from the main roads. Clean toilets will be found at most places, large or small. Another step forward has been the rising standard of cafés outside of the cities catering for travellers. While food is generally more healthy and appetising these days, many cafés confirmed that ownership of an espresso machine doesn't guarantee competency in its use. Stick with major coffee brands like Illy, Atomic, Vittorio or L'Affare and you won't go too wrong.

North Island Routes

		Page
1	Auckland – Dargaville SH 16, 11, 19, 24	10
2	Dargaville – Kaitaia via Hokianga Harbour, SH 12	14
3	Kaitaia – Cape Reinga SH 1	16
4	Whangarei – Kaitaia via Bay of Islands and Doubtless Bay SH 1, 11, 10	18
5	Auckland – Whangarei SH 1	22
6	Whangarei – Kaitaia SH 1	22
7	Auckland – Hamilton SH 1	24
8	Auckland – Waiuku – Raglan SH 22	24
9	Auckland – Thames SH 1, 2, 25	26
10	Coromandel Peninsula SH 25, 25a	28
11	Auckland – Rotorua SH 1, 2, 27, 5	32
12	Auckland – Taupo SH 2, 27, 1	32
13	Rotorua – Taupo SH 5	32
14	Hamilton – Kawhia SH 23, 31	34
15	Hamilton – New Plymouth SH 3	34
16	Hamilton – Tirau SH 1	36
16a	Hamilton – Taupo via Pureora Forest SH 3, 30, 1	36
17	Hamilton – Wanganui SH 4	38
18	Taumarunui – Turangi SH 41	40
19	Taumarunui – Stratford SH 43	42
20	Waihi – Opotiki SH 2	44
21	Opotiki – Gisborne SH 35	46
22	Opotiki – Gisborne via Waioeka Gorge SH 2	48
23	Gisborne – Wairoa SH 2	52
24	Gisborne – Wairoa via Tiniroto SH 6	52
25	Wairoa – Napier SH 2	54
26	Rotorua – Waikaremoana – Wairoa SH 5, 38	56
27	Rotorua – Whakatane SH 30	58
28	New Plymouth – Hawera SH 45	60
29	New Plymouth – Bulls SH 3	62
30	Bulls – Wellington SH 1	64
31	Taupo – Bulls SH 1	66
32	Taupo – Napier SH 5	68
33	Napier/Hastings – Palmerston North SH 2,3	70
34	Woodville – Wellington SH 2	72

Cape Reinga

3

Kaitaia

4

2

5

4

5

Whangarei

2

6

Dargaville

1

6

1

Auckland

9

Thames

10

8

Waihi

7

11

20

Tauranga

20

Hamilton

16

Whakatane

14

11

27

21

Te Kuiti

12

Rotorua

Opotiki

15

16a

13

22

26

17

16

Taupo

24

Taumarunui

18

Gisborne

New Plymouth

19

Turangi

32

23

29

25

Wairoa

28

17

Hawera

31

Napier

29

Wanganui

33

29

Bulls

Palmerston North

Woodville

30

34

Masterton

34

Wellington

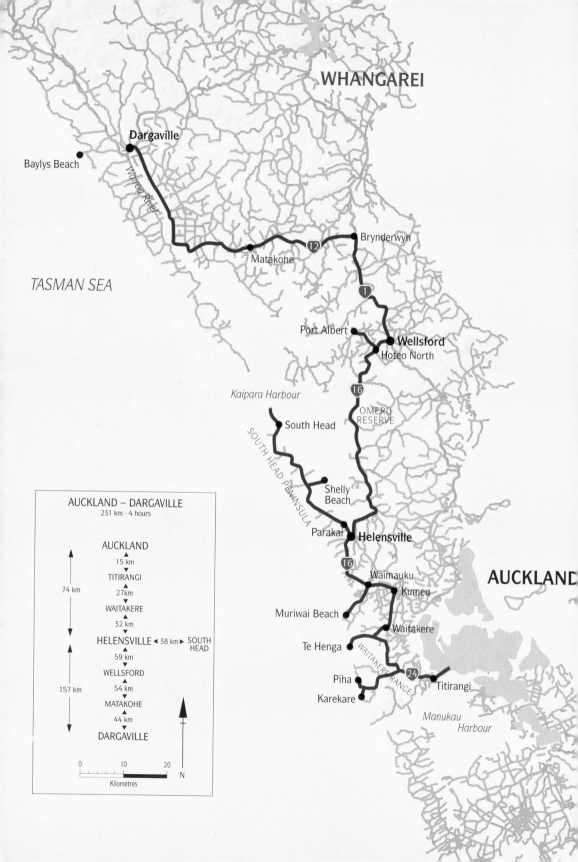

WHANGAREI

Dargaville

Baylys Beach

Wairoa River

TASMAN SEA

Matakohe

12

Brynderwyn

1

Port Albert

Wellsford

Hoteo North

16

OMERU
RESERVE

Kaipara Harbour

South Head

SOUTH HEAD PENINSULA

Shelly
Beach

Parakai

Helensville

16

Waimauku

Kumeu

AUCKLAND

Muriwai Beach

Waitakere

Te Henga

WAITAKERE RANGE

24

Titirangi

Piha

Karekare

Manukau
Harbour

AUCKLAND – DARGAVILLE
231 km · 4 hours

AUCKLAND
▲
15 km
TITIRANGI
▲
27km
WAITAKERE
▲
32 km
HELENSVILLE ◄ 38 km ► SOUTH
HEAD
59 km
WELLSFORD
▲
54 km
MATAKOHE
▲
44 km
DARGAVILLE

74 km

157 km

0   10   20
Kilometres

N

Northland

Northland is highly under-rated by international visitors who for the most part head south the minute they land in Auckland. This is a shame, because Northland's attractions – a combination of rich human history and extraordinary coastal and forest scenery – are such that it stands apart from many other regions. Much can be learned about early Maori and European social and cultural history, which is evident in the many marae, pa, colonial buildings and the historically significant Waitangi National Reserve in the Bay of Islands.

Drivers are well catered for by Northland's 'Twin Coast Discovery Highway' route. Although the awkward title suggests a single continuous road, the 'highway' is in fact a combination of major and secondary roads (all sealed and in good order) that describe a circular journey around Northland from Auckland. The highway thus links the major west Auckland and Northland attractions: the Waitakere Range and west coast beaches at Piha, Bethells Beach and Muriwai; the kauri forests; Kaipara and Hokianga harbours; Cape Reinga; Doubtless Bay; the Bay of Islands and the sublime coastal resorts in the Waipu/Mangawhai/Warkworth areas.

The Discovery Highway is described here in three sections – Auckland to Kaitaia via the west coast, Kaitaia–Cape Reinga, and Auckland–Kaitaia via the east coast. SH 1, the major route north from Auckland, generally lacks the charms of the coastal routes though it is useful as quick access to different parts of Northland. For notes on SH 1 see the eastern section. Many tourists head straight up to the Bay of Islands and then cut west to Hokianga Harbour and Waipoua Forest via Kaikohe. However, if you have time, the complete circuit of Northland on the Discovery Highway route is well rewarded – up the west and down the east is my recommendation. Worth getting from visitor centres is the Department of Conservation pamphlet on Northland conservation camping areas.

Discovery Highway (Western Section)
Auckland–Dargaville–Hokianga Harbour–Kaitaia

Auckland–Dargaville SH 16, 11, 19, 24
231 km, 4 hours
From central Auckland travel west on SH 16 (motorway) and exit at Waterview/Great North Road, then follow SH 11, 19 and then 24 to Titirangi (good cafés here).

Waitakere Range – campgrounds, walks, swimming, surfing, fishing
The Discovery Highway offers fine views over Auckland as it wends its way along SH 24 through leafy Titirangi and up into the forested Waitakere Range. About 10 km from Titirangi is the Arataki Visitor Centre where you'll find information about the area's natural and human history, and the numerous coast and forest walks – get hold of the free Waitakere Ranges Regional Park brochure for information on these. 10 km from the centre is the turnoff to Piha, one of three impressive surf beaches accessed on this section from SH 24. The other beaches are Karekare Beach (made famous by *The Piano*) also reached from the Piha road, and Te Henga (Bethells Beach) reached from a turnoff down Te Henga Road near Waitakere village. Cafés on this section are located at the Piha Road junction and at Piha Beach.

Kumeu

SH 24 ends at Kumeu where the Discovery Highway rejoins SH 16. A little way south of Kumeu on SH 16 are several notable wine producers: Nobilos, Selaks and Coopers Creek, each offering cafés and winetasting. In Kumeu, Girasol Café at the north end of the town offers great travellers' food, while 2 km north of here is the more upmarket but very good Bees On Line organic honey centre and café. Five kilometres north of Kumeu at Waimauku is the turnoff to Muriwai Beach (10 km) where the highlights are New Zealand's northernmost Australasian gannet colony, fur seals, a great coastal walkway, swimming and surfing.

Helensville

The Discovery Highway reaches the southern end of Kaipara Harbour at Helensville where you'll get good food (ranging from wholesome to wicked) and coffee at the Ginger Crunch Café. The Regent Café is another good eatery here. A worthwhile side journey is along the South Head Peninsula (45 minutes to South Head from Helensville on a sealed road) with fine views, swimming at Shelly Beach and Mosquito Bay, sea and freshwater fishing, hot pools at Parakai and the café MacNut Farms Macadamia Farm.

Kaipara Harbour

From Helensville the Discovery Highway (still on SH 16) follows the Kaipara River then turns inland and works around Kaipara Harbour. Several small reserves offer picnic sites and walks along the way. Omeru Reserve (signposted 18 km from Helensville) contains a Maori pa site, and a stand of tall totara and kauri; Port Albert is the site of an historic settlement on the edge of Kaipara Harbour 8 km from SH 16 (turn off 1.6 km north of Hoteo North). It's a pleasant, quiet spot for lunch, with camping and toilet facilities. A highpoint overlooking the harbour is reached before the descent towards Wellsford where the Discovery Highway links briefly with SH 1.

Kaiwaka

Kaiwaka is notable for its Northland regional information centre, and the Eutopia Organic Café.

Matakohe

North of Wellsford, turn west at Brynderwyn onto SH 12 and drive 26 km to Matakohe where the famous Matakohe kauri museum is located. Here, in displays (including working displays of mill and other equipment), exhibits and photographs, the story is told of the unrelenting logging of Northland's kauri forests through the nineteenth and early twentieth centuries. Allow at least a couple of hours here then drive away and marvel at how hard the pioneer loggers, millers, farmers and road builders had to work to create the landscape before you. You might then reflect on how little of the old forest remains, and be thankful that New Zealand's earliest conservationists succeeded in preserving any of Northland's forest at all.

Dargaville – campground

At Dargaville on the north bank of the wide and muddy Wairoa River the maritime museum is worth a visit and the Blah Blah Blah Café offers good food and coffee. However, the choice eatery in the area is the Funky Fish Café at the magnificent Baylys Beach 15 km west of Dargaville (turn off SH 12, 4 km from the town centre). From Dargaville the Discovery Highway continues up SH 12, but SH 14 offers a quick (1 hour) route to Whangarei for those travelling east.

Dargaville–Kaitaia via Hokianga Harbour SH 12
189 km, 4 hours

This leg of the Discovery Highway is equal to anywhere on the South Island's West Coast. By the fastest route (via Kaikohe and SH 1), Dargaville to Kaitaia can be travelled in just over three hours, but there's little point in doing that. Allow a day, drive slowly, enjoy the walks at Trounson Kauri Park and Waipoua Forest, then catch the vehicle ferry from Rawene across Hokianga Harbour and follow the back roads to Ahipara and Kaitaia.

Trounson Kauri Park – campground, walks, picnicking

Trounson is down a well-marked side road off SH 12, 30 km north of Dargaville. (If coming from the

Tane Mahuta, Waipoua Forest

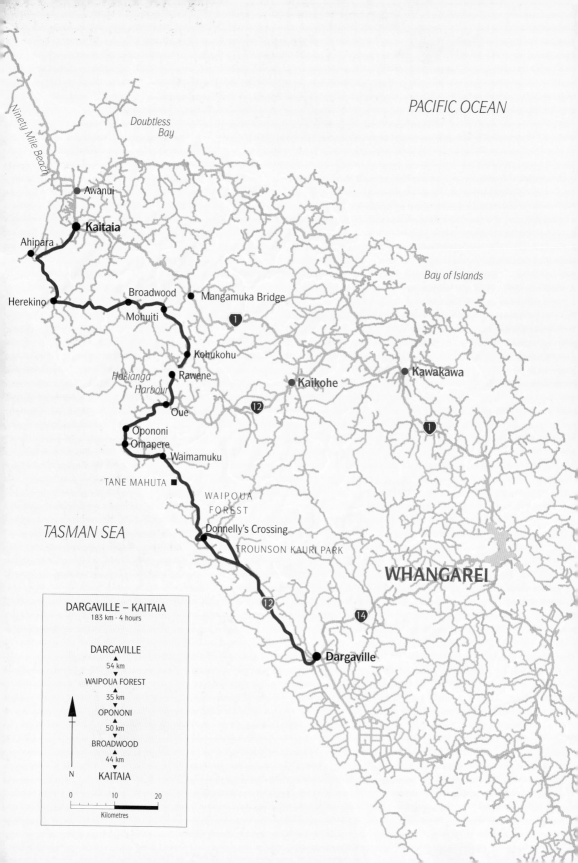

PACIFIC OCEAN

Ninety Mile Beach

Doubtless Bay

Awanui

Kaitaia

Ahipara

Bay of Islands

Herekino

Broadwood

Mangamuka Bridge

Mohuiti

①

Kohukohu

Rawene

Kawakawa

Hokianga Harbour

Kaikohe

Oue

⑫

①

Opononi

Omapere

Waimamuku

TANE MAHUTA ■

WAIPOUA FOREST

TASMAN SEA

Donnelly's Crossing

TROUNSON KAURI PARK

WHANGAREI

⑫

⑭

Dargaville

DARGAVILLE – KAITAIA
183 km · 4 hours

DARGAVILLE
▲
54 km
▼
WAIPOUA FOREST
▲
35 km
▼
OPONONI
▲
50 km
▼
BROADWOOD
▲
44 km
▼
KAITAIA

N

0   10   20
Kilometres

north, an unsealed road to the park via Donnelly's Crossing leaves SH 12 about 6 km from the Waipoua Forest Visitor Centre). This large (573 ha) forest remnant contains some superb kauri, viewed from an easy 40-minute loop track suitable for all ages and even those in wheelchairs. Despite the cheesy poetry dressed up as natural history interpretation, one can learn much about kauri and other forest trees and wildlife on this walk. The Department of Conservation manages the area as a 'mainland island,' which involves intensive predator and weed control, so what you experience is a very healthy native forest and kiwi habitat compared with other forests in the region.

Waipoua Forest – campground, walks

Flanked by huge kauri, rata, kohekohe and other large trees, the almost 20 km drive through Waipoua Forest is the highlight of the western section of the Discovery Highway. The park was created in 1952, and its natural and social history are described at the visitor centre which arguably offers a more balanced view of Northland's logging and gumdigging past than other places. A lookout 3 km south of the centre offers a fine view, while the easy five-minute walk (8 km north of the centre) to Tane Mahuta, the largest known kauri, is a 'must do'.

Hokianga Harbour

Continuing north, petrol can be bought at Waimamaku soon after Waipoua Forest, then Hokianga Harbour appears unexpectedly, beyond a rise with a view across the harbour to an enormous dune on its north bank. From here the road descends to the harbourside settlements of Omapere and Opononi. Families will enjoy Omapere's Amazing Maize Maze, five minutes drive from the village off the road to the Waterfall Track, while the information centre at Opononi has good information about Hokianga attractions and history. Shortly after Oue, the Discovery Highway turns left off SH 12 and makes for Rawene (Kaikohe is a 45-minute drive on SH 12 for those who want to travel east to SH 1). At Rawene the ferry to Kohukohu ($14 for car and driver, and $2 per passenger) departs on the half-hour (from Kohukohu it leaves on the hour). A walk on Rawene's mangrove forest boardwalk, a bite to eat at the Boathouse Café or a stroll amongst the village's colonial buildings (Clendon House) are pleasant ways to pass time waiting for the ferry.

Kohukohu–Kaitaia (74 km)

Kohukohu has a historic walk that takes in the village's colonial homes and buildings (the new Waterline Café is recommended here). From Kohukohu the Discovery Highway takes you north along the edge of Hokianga Harbour before an enjoyable drive west through farmland and regenerating forest, past Broadwood and Herekino, towards Ahipara at the bottom of Ninety Mile Beach and the turnoff to Kaitaia. Alternately, you may drive east to SH 1 from Mohuiti to Mangamuka Bridge.

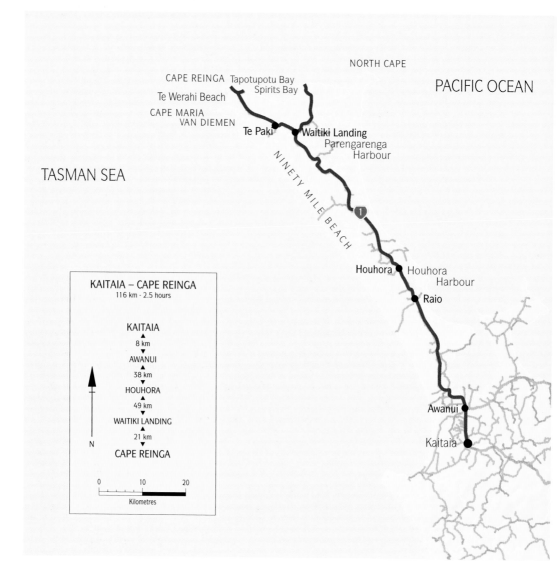

NORTH CAPE

PACIFIC OCEAN

CAPE REINGA Tapotupotu Bay
Spirits Bay
Te Werahi Beach
CAPE MARIA
VAN DIEMEN
Te Paki Waitiki Landing
Parengarenga
Harbour

TASMAN SEA

NINETY MILE BEACH

Houhora Houhora
Harbour
Raio

Awanui

Kaitaia

KAITAIA – CAPE REINGA
116 km · 2.5 hours

KAITAIA
▲
8 km
▼
AWANUI
▲
38 km
▼
HOUHORA
▲
49 km
▼
WAITIKI LANDING
▲
21 km
▼
CAPE REINGA

N

0   10   20
Kilometres

Kaitaia–Cape Reinga SH 1
116 km, 2.5 hours

The Discovery Highway reaches its northern point at Cape Reinga. The drive takes in pleasant Northland farmland for much of the way, crossing flats north of Kaitaia, and into more undulating grass-covered dunes and pine plantations further north with fine views over Parengarenga Harbour before Waitiki Landing.

Awanui
Big River Café (on the SH 1/SH 10 intersection), with great food, coffee and friendly staff, is a good breakfast or brunch option for those leaving Kaitaia early for the Cape or heading over to Doubtless Bay. Awanui's Ancient Kauri Kingdom features giant kauri logs, crafts and furniture, and also has a café.

Houhora Harbour – campground
Just south of Raio is a signposted turnoff to the Waggener Park Museum and campground, sited idyllically on the edge of Houhora Harbour. There's little to tempt taste buds at the café here, though the museum will attract those with an interest in pioneer-era artefacts.

Waitiki Landing
After climbing to a high dune ridge with views of Parengarenga Harbour's inlets and mangrove forests, the road reaches Waitiki Landing where there is a store, petrol and accommodation and information.

Cape Reinga – walks, views
The last 21 km to Cape Reinga from Waitiki Landing should be driven with care as it climbs and winds through regenerating scrublands and forests, and distinctive outcrops and cuttings of red volcanic rock. Shortly before the carpark at Cape Reinga is a turnoff to Tapotupotu Bay (picnic site and campground).

Cape Reinga, the lighthouse and views across extensive dunelands and remote clifflines are the main attractions at the road end. A short walk north leads to the lighthouse. The Cape is particularly significant in Maori spiritual belief as the place where the spirits of their dead depart for Hawaiiki – the home of their ancestors. Eastwards on a fine day is a view toward North Cape while northwards the Tasman Sea and the Pacific Ocean crash together in foamy swells and lines of waves over the Columbia Bank. Below the carpark to the south is Te Werahi Beach and Cape Maria van Diemen.

Cape walks
A turnoff west at Te Paki (about 6 km from Waitiki Landing) down Te Paki Stream Road leads to stunning dune walks from the road end (picnic site) towards Ninety Mile Beach. Similarly, a 30-minute dune walk from Te Werahi Gate leads to Te Werahi Beach and impressive coastal scenery in the vicinity of Cape Maria van Diemen. At Cape Reinga, walks lead to Te Werahi Beach and Tapotupotu Bay. Information on these walks (and the Te Paki Farm Park which encompasses much of the Cape Reinga area) can be found at the DoC office at Te Paki.

Waitiki Landing–Spirits Bay
From Waitiki Landing a winding unsealed road through a Muriwhenua Incorporation forestry area leads to Spirits Bay where there is a DoC campground and wild beach. The drive offers excellent views of Parengarenga Harbour before the steep descent to Spirits Bay.

NB: Driving Ninety Mile Beach is not recommended for ordinary vehicles. Bus tours are the safest way to experience this stretch of coast.

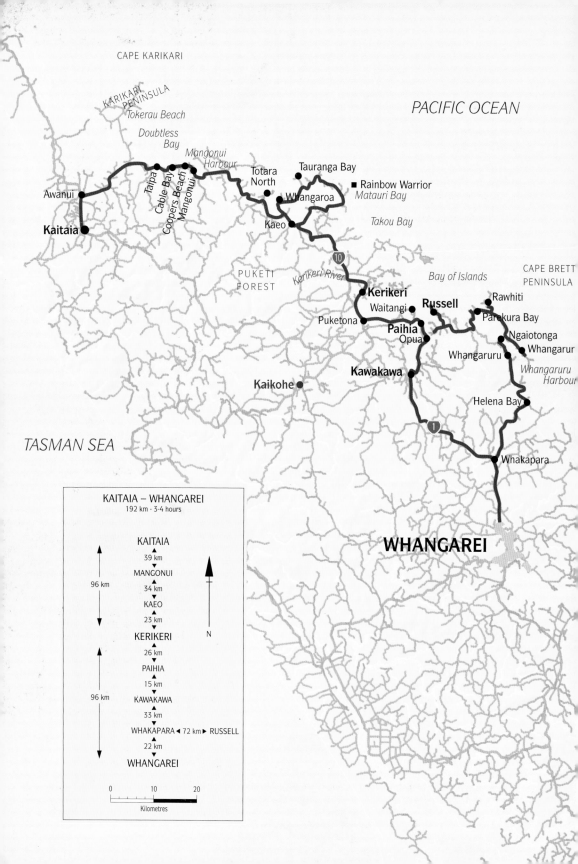

CAPE KARIKARI

KARIKARI PENINSULA

Tokerau Beach

Doubtless Bay

Mangonui Harbour

PACIFIC OCEAN

Awanui

Taipa
Cable Bay
Coopers Beach
Mangonui

Kaitaia

Totara North

Tauranga Bay

Whangaroa

■ Rainbow Warrior
Matauri Bay

Kaeo

Takou Bay

PUKETI FOREST

Kerikeri River

(10)

Kerikeri

Waitangi

Puketona

Paihia
Opua

Kawakawa

Kaikohe

Bay of Islands

Russell

Rawhiti

Parekura Bay

Ngaiotonga

Whangarur

Whangaruru

Whangaruru Harbour

CAPE BRETT PENINSULA

Helena Bay

(1)

Whakapara

WHANGAREI

TASMAN SEA

KAITAIA – WHANGAREI
192 km · 3-4 hours

96 km

▲ KAITAIA ▼
39 km
▲ MANGONUI ▼
34 km
▲ KAEO ▼
23 km
▲ KERIKERI ▼
26 km
▲ PAIHIA ▼
15 km
▲ KAWAKAWA ▼
33 km
▲ WHAKAPARA ◄ 72 km ► RUSSELL
22 km
▼ WHANGAREI

96 km

96 km

N

0   10   20

Kilometres

Discovery Highway (Eastern Section)
Whangarei–Kaitaia via Bay of Islands and Doubtless Bay SH 1, 11, 10
192 km, 3–4 hours

Northland's sublime east coast beaches and coastal resorts are in direct contrast with the forests, harbours and lesser-developed character of the west. The route described follows the 'Twin Coast Discovery Highway' from Whangarei through the Bay of Islands and Doubtless Bay.

SH 1 (Whakapara)–Russell via Whangaruru Harbour (1 hour)
A highly recommended alternative route to Russell and Paihia is this scenic drive that takes in the eastern Bay of Islands' bays, inlets, forests and Whangaruru Harbour. Remote beaches and camping sites are a feature of the drive, with plenty of ways to fill in a day pottering down roads for rewarding walks and scenery. From Whakapara, drive to Helena Bay. Continue on and take the turnoff toward to Ngaiotonga. (The diversion southeast from Ngaiotonga to Whangaruru North Head – location of a popular campsite – is rewarded with a 90-minute (return) walk to the head for outstanding views.) From Ngaiotonga continue to the base of Cape Brett Peninsula. You can turn here to Rawhiti and the beginning of the Cape Brett Track. Otherwise follow the winding route past Parekura Bay to Russell.

Russell – campground, walks, swimming, fishing
As well as occupying a significant place in New Zealand's early European history, Russell is a major holiday spot and headquarters of the Bay of Islands' Maritime and Historical Park. A number of historic buildings and the Russell Museum are of note. Of the cafés the York St Café is recommended here. Continue to Paihia on the ferry service to Opua (runs every ten minutes from Okiato – see Opua/Paihia/Waitangi section below for timetable details).

Kawakawa
Kawakawa is 45 minutes from Whangarei. The main reason people stop at Kawakawa is to admire (and use!) the famous public toilet created for the town by the German architect and artist Frederick Hundertwasser. Of the café options, Café Tuna on SH 1 at Moerewa just north of the town is recommended, otherwise there's Trainspotters in the town centre.

Opua/Paihia/Waitangi
Opua, about an hour from Whangarei, is reached by turning off SH 1 at Kawakawa onto SH 11. The main interest at Opua is the

Paihia, Bay of Islands

vehicle ferry to Russell which departs every 10 minutes between 6.50 a.m. and 10 p.m. in summer and until 8.45 p.m. in winter. The coastal forest walk through Harrison Scenic Reserve (30 minutes) at Opua is highly recommended.

Paihia, 6 km from Opua, has several good cafés and places to swim or picnic. At the busy waterfront information centre you can organise bay cruises, fishing, dolphin and whale-watching.

Waitangi National Reserve is one of the country's outstanding historic reserves. Here in 1840, New Zealand's founding document, the Treaty of Waitangi, was signed by Maori and the British Crown. Audiovisual presentations and historical displays at the reserve's visitor centre, and the *son et lumière* in the Whare Runanga (meeting house) are highlights of a visit here. Although the presentations skirt contemporary grievances against the treaty, and say little about how Maori were treated thereafter, they offer nonetheless a valuable introduction to New Zealand history. There is a café, and opportunity for walks in the Treaty Grounds and to nearby Haruru Falls.

From Waitangi many travellers cut west to the kauri forests via Ohaeawai and Kaikohe (allow a couple of hours to reach Hokianga Harbour – see Route 1). To continue north to Kerikeri head for the SH 10 junction at Puketona).

Kerikeri – campground, walks, picnicking

Kerikeri township (26 km from Waitangi) lies on the Kerikeri River in the Bay of Islands. Renowned for

its Maori and European settler history, it is also a centre for crafts, culture and kiwifruit. Below the township in Kerikeri Basin is Kemp House, a former mission station built between 1821 and 1822, the oldest standing building in the country. Nearby is the Stone Store, a fine example of nineteenth-century stonemasonry completed in 1835, while on the hill behind Kemp House is the weatherboard St James Church, dating from 1878. Remains of the once heavily pallisaded Kororipo Pa can be reached by a short interpreted walk from the Stone Store. Opposite Kemp House is Rewa's village, a re-creation of an unfortified village that stood on the site in the nineteenth century. Kerikeri has numerous eateries and bars but the Rocket Café close to the SH 10 junction

Stone Store and St James Church, Kerikeri south of the town centre stands out for its coffee and good food.

Matauri Bay – campground, fishing

About 17 km from Kerikeri is the turnoff to Matauri Bay, a settlement populated by Nga Puhi who own and run the popular holiday park there. On the headland overlooking the bay is the striking memorial to the Rainbow Warrior – icon of New Zealand's anti-nuclear advocacy in the 1980s. The boat, bombed by French government agents in Auckland in 1986, now rests on the seabed off the Cavalli Islands northeast of here. The short climb to the memorial by sculptor Chris Booth is a pilgrimage everyone should make. The views from the scenic drive between Matauri Bay and Whangaroa Harbour make it a worthwhile option for returning to SH 10 if you have time. Allow an hour to reach Whangaroa.

Kaeo – walking

Kaeo services the surrounding farming and horticultural area. Janit's Texas Diner, styled after US 'road-houses', has a good reputation for those in need of steak, while its home-cooked cakes look a treat. 16 km west of Kaeo is Puketi Forest which can be accessed from Waiare Road (turnoff south of Kaeo, unsealed). The Puketi Nature Trail involves a 1 hour loop through kauri/podocarp forest which also protects rare birds such as the kaka and kokako.

Whangaroa Harbour – campground, swimming, fishing

The scenic and sheltered Whangaroa Harbour is reached from a turnoff about 5 km from Kaeo. The harbour is surrounded by steep hills and volcanic plugs including the prominent St Paul on the skyline opposite Whangaroa above Totara North. The harbour is a deep-sea fishing base, and harbour cruises are popular. Unfortunately a controversial marine farm has wrecked the view of the harbour on the drive to the settlement. Tauranga Bay east of the harbour has a great beach and campground.

Doubtless Bay – swimming, fishing

From Whangaroa Harbour the road climbs then descends to the pohutukawa-lined beaches of Doubtless Bay. The wharf at Mangonui remains a popular fishing spot, though locals claim (as they seem to everywhere) 'the fishing isn't as good as it was'. Mangonui's Waterfront Café and the Slung Anchor Bar offer two good eating options. Further along SH 10 is the sublime Coopers Beach, followed in quick succession by Cable Bay and Taipa. Tokerau Beach (store, toilets) on the Karikari Peninsula is reached from an intersection about 8 km from Taipa. Also worth visiting on the peninsula is Matai Bay (unsealed for the last few kilometres, fine sheltered beaches and a great DoC campground), and Rangiputa at the mouth of Rangaunu Harbour – a wild and beautiful spot.

Motuarohia Island, Bay of Islands

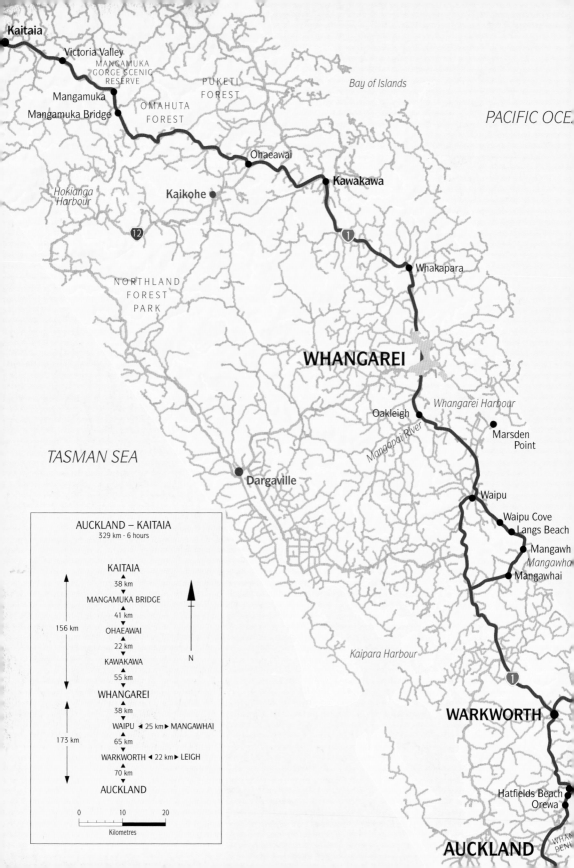

Kaitaia

Victoria Valley

MANGAMUKA
GORGE SCENIC
RESERVE

Mangamuka

Mangamuka Bridge

OMAHUTA
FOREST

PUKETI
FOREST

Bay of Islands

PACIFIC OCE...

Ohaeawai

Kawakawa

Kaikohe

*Hokianga
Harbour*

12

1

Whakapara

NORTHLAND
FOREST
PARK

WHANGAREI

Whangarei Harbour

Oakleigh

Marsden
Point

Mangapai River

TASMAN SEA

Dargaville

Waipu

Waipu Cove
Langs Beach

Mangawh...
Mangawho...

Mangawhai

Kaipara Harbour

1

WARKWORTH

Hatfields Beach
Orewa

AUCKLAND

WHAN...
PEN...

AUCKLAND – KAITAIA
329 km · 6 hours

KAITAIA
▲ ▼ 38 km
MANGAMUKA BRIDGE
▲ ▼ 41 km
156 km   OHAEAWAI
▲ ▼ 22 km
KAWAKAWA
▲ ▼ 55 km
WHANGAREI
▲ ▼ 38 km
WAIPU ◄ 25 km ► MANGAWHAI
▲ ▼ 65 km
173 km   WARKWORTH ◄ 22 km ► LEIGH
▲ ▼ 70 km
AUCKLAND

N

0   10   20
Kilometres

Auckland–Whangarei SH 1
173 km, 3 hours

Hatfields Beach, Orewa, Waiwera Springs
Seaside resorts at Hatfields Beach, Orewa and the popular Waiwera thermal springs are the first of the highlights on the route north from Auckland. Those in exploratory mood should drive out to the beaches of Whangaparaoa Peninsula. Shakespear Regional Park on the peninsula's eastern extremity is open to the public for walks and camping.

Warkworth
Boutique wineries, cafés, an art and craft trail, and numerous attractive beaches are features of the Warkworth area. A trip to Leigh and to the Goat Island Marine Reserve (24 km) is one of the highlights – snorkelling and diving in the 'no fishing' reserve is often rewarded with remarkable encounters with large snapper and moki. The Sawmill Café, just out of Leigh towards the reserve, is an excellent establishment, while in Warkworth visit the Queen St Corner Café.

Waipu environs – campground, walks, swimming, fishing
Seekers of beaches and coastal scenery should leave SH 1 on a signposted scenic route 7 km after Wellsford (or alternatively and quicker, turnoff at Kaiwaka) and head for Mangawhai Heads, Langs Beach and Waipu Cove. The beaches are excellent and holidaymakers are well catered for. Recommended cafés in the area include The Smashed Pipi at Mangawhai, and the Naja Garden Café at Mangawhai Heads. The Mangawhai Cliffs Walkway from Mangawhai Heads is a recommended walk in this area. Return to SH 1 at Waipu.

For those interested in visiting New Zealand's sole oil refinery, the turnoff to Marsden Point is 21 km from a turnoff at Ruakaka.

Whangarei–Kaitaia SH 1
156 km, 3 hours

This is the quick route from Whangarei to Hokianga Harbour, the Bay of Islands and Kaitaia, however the road is often busier, and generally lacks the charms of the east and west coast drives. Petrol and other services are available at most centres. At Ohaeawai is the turnoff for SH 12 to Kaikohe (12 km), the kauri forests and Dargaville; while a turnoff at Mangamuka Bridge provides quick access to the northern Hokianga Harbour. Scenic highlights of the route are the views across Puketi and Omahuta forests before Mangamuka Bridge, and the crossing of the Mangamuka Gorge Scenic Reserve.

Hauraki Gulf

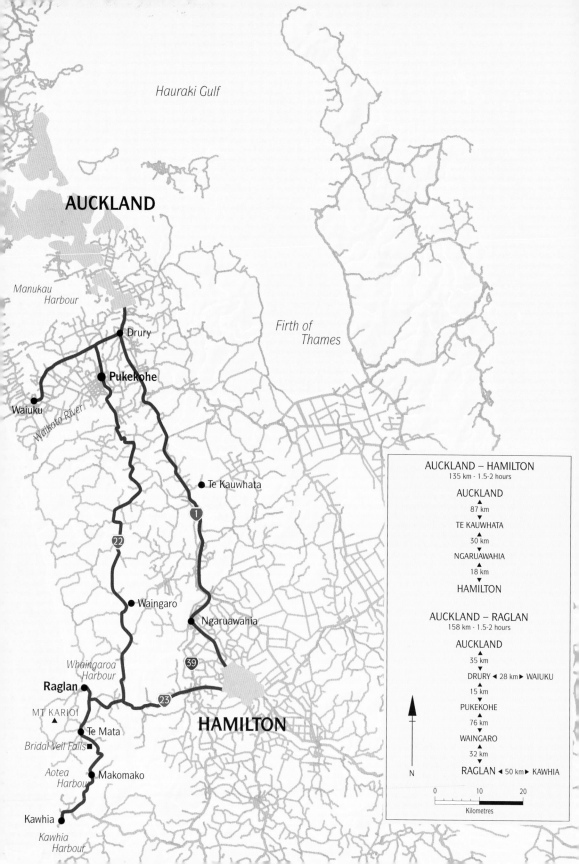

Hauraki Gulf

AUCKLAND

Manukau Harbour

Drury

Pukekohe

Waiuku

Waikato River

Firth of Thames

Te Kauwhata

1

22

Waingaro

Ngaruawahia

39

Whaingaroa Harbour

Raglan

23

MT KARIOI

Te Mata

Bridal Veil Falls

HAMILTON

Aotea Harbour

Makomako

Kawhia

Kawhia Harbour

AUCKLAND – HAMILTON
135 km · 1.5-2 hours

AUCKLAND
▲
87 km
▼
TE KAUWHATA
▲
30 km
▼
NGARUAWAHIA
▲
18 km
▼
HAMILTON

AUCKLAND – RAGLAN
158 km · 1.5-2 hours

AUCKLAND
▲
35 km
▼
DRURY ◄ 28 km ► WAIUKU
▲
15 km
▼
PUKEKOHE
▲
76 km
▼
WAINGARO
▲
32 km
▼
RAGLAN ◄ 50 km ► KAWHIA

N

0   10   20
Kilometres

Auckland–Hamilton SH 1
135 km, 1.5–2 hours

The drive to Hamilton down SH 1 involves one of the busiest stretches of road in New Zealand. Consequently, there's no shortage of places to refuel or find a meal at any of the centres *en route*. Wineries at Te Kauwhata (87 km from Auckland) include the Rongopai winery which has a pleasant café. Huntly's coal mining museum is worth a visit, while a kilometre south of Ngaruawahia is the pleasant Country Café. The SH 39 turnoff to Otorohanga (68 km to Otorohanga) is useful to note as it offers a bypass around Hamilton and access to Raglan and Kawhia harbours.

Auckland–Waiuku–Raglan via Pukekohe SH 22
158 km, 1.5–2 hours

This route to Raglan is more scenic and the roads are quieter than travel via SH 1 and Hamilton. To reach Pukekohe, leave the Auckland motorway at Drury and turn onto SH 22. The route then follows SH 22 until it meets SH 23, 14 km east of Raglan.

Waiuku/Awhitu Peninsula – campground, swimming, picnicking
Waiuku (28 km from Drury, 50 minutes from central Auckland), a charming rural town at the base of the Awhitu Peninsula on the edge of Manukau Harbour, is worth visiting for its historic buildings, pioneer museum and beaches and campgrounds on the peninsula.

Pukekohe–Raglan
108 km, 1.5 hours
Pukekohe (50 km from Auckland) is a bustling town servicing the surrounding market gardening region. The drive to Raglan winds through undulating plains and hill country and occasional forest remnants including a fine stand of totara at St Albans near Waingaro. Hot springs at Waingaro have been developed into an attractive spa – a fun place for families, with an adjacent motorcamp and tavern. The last few kilometres to the SH 23 junction are unsealed.

Raglan – campground, walks, swimming, surfing, picnicking, fishing
Raglan is a justly popular holiday resort on the edge of Whaingaroa Harbour. Renowned (among other things) for its surf beaches, kite surfing, orca, and its stone symposium, the settlement has a laid back holiday feel, and its residents have made a strong commitment to turning their village into an environmentally friendly locale. There are several good cafés on the main street: Tongue in Groove, Department of Food and Aqua Velvet. Walks to Mt Karioi from the coast (allow 4–5 hours) and the Bridal Veil Falls (20 minutes return) near Te Mata are popular, as is the Te Toto Gorge Track – these are described in a DoC brochure available at the Raglan visitor centre. The 50 km 'back route' to Kawhia along Raglan Road via Te Mata and Makomako is a recommended scenic drive though it is two-thirds unsealed and requires care, particularly on narrower sections at the Kawhia end. Allow an hour from Raglan to reach Hamilton along SH 23.

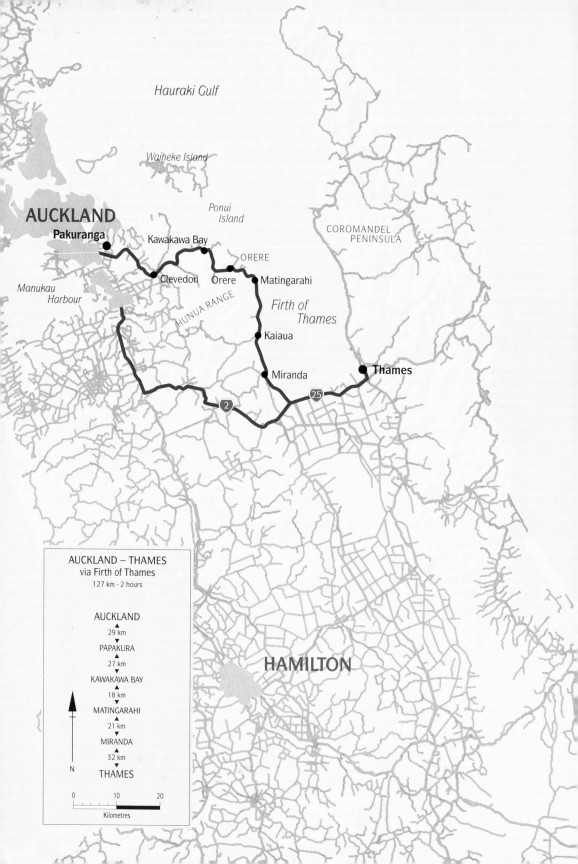

Hauraki Gulf

Waiheke Island

Ponui Island

AUCKLAND

Pakuranga

Kawakawa Bay

ORERE

Clevedon

Orere

Matingarahi

Manukau Harbour

COROMANDEL PENINSULA

HUNUA RANGE

Firth of Thames

Kaiaua

Miranda

Thames

25

2

HAMILTON

AUCKLAND – THAMES
via Firth of Thames
127 km - 2 hours

AUCKLAND
▲ 29 km ▼
PAPAKURA
▲ 27 km ▼
KAWAKAWA BAY
▲ 18 km ▼
MATINGARAHI
▲ 21 km ▼
MIRANDA
▲ 32 km ▼
THAMES

N

0   10   20
Kilometres

Auckland–Thames SH 1, 2, 25
115 km, 90 minutes

The quickest route from Auckland to Thames is via SH 1, 2 and 25 and takes 90 minutes on a good traffic-less day without delays at Kohu Bridge near Thames. If you take this route you have the option of cutting directly to Miranda (see below) by taking a turn left off SH 2 (signposted) just after Mangatawhiri.

The SH 25 turnoff to Thames via Waitakaruru is 35 km from the SH 1 exit on the Auckland-Hamilton Expressway. Mangatawhiri's Chateau Crème Delight sells great ice creams. The Black Beagle Café a kilometre past Maramarua is another potential place for a break.

Auckland–Thames via Pakuranga, Firth of Thames coast, SH 25
127 km, 2 hours

I'd recommend the slightly longer scenic drive to Thames from Pakuranga that skirts along the Firth of Thames and the base of the Hunua Range. Leave the SH 1 motorway south of Auckland at the Pakuranga exit and turn left towards Pakuranga and follow signs toward Clevedon and Hunua.

At Kawakawa Bay views spread north to Waiheke and Ponui Islands. The road climbs through the forests of Te Morehu Scenic Reserve to Orere and the Orere Point campground. The road narrows between Matingarahi and Kaiaua (apparently the best fish and chips in New Zealand here).

Miranda's Shorebird Centre is the first port of call for exploring the internationally important wading bird reserve in the firth's tidal shallows across the road, one of several locations in New Zealand where Northern Hemisphere migratory species congregate to escape the northern winter. There is walking access to the firth opposite the centre, and about 2 km further south (from a signposted rest area through land covenanted with the Queen Elizabeth II Trust) — at both places please respect the fact that you are crossing private land. Miranda's other attraction is its natural hot springs located at a holiday park/campground south of the shorebird centre.

West coast, Coromandel Peninsula

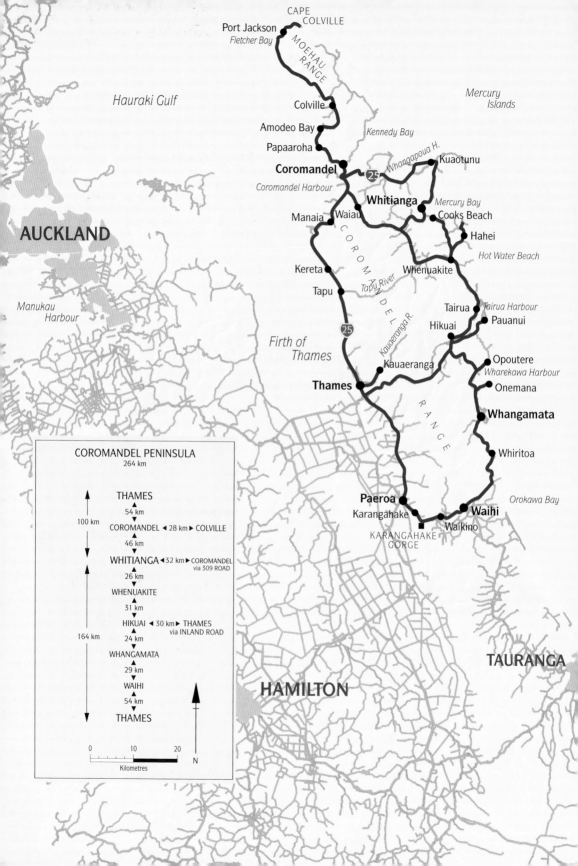

CAPE
COLVILLE

Port Jackson
Fletcher Bay

MOEHAU RANGE

Hauraki Gulf

Mercury Islands

Colville

Amodeo Bay

Kennedy Bay

Papaaroha

Coromandel

Whangapoua H.

Kuaotunu

(25)

Coromandel Harbour

Whitianga

Mercury Bay

Manaia

Waiau

Cooks Beach

AUCKLAND

Hahei

Hot Water Beach

Kereta

Tapu River

Whenuakite

Tapu

Manukau Harbour

C O R O M A N D E L

Tairua

Tairua Harbour

Pauanui

Hikuai

(25)

Kauaeranga R.

Firth of Thames

Kauaeranga

Opoutere

Wharekawa Harbour

Onemana

Thames

Whangamata

R A N G E

Whiritoa

Paeroa

Orokawa Bay

Karangahake

Waihi

COROMANDEL PENINSULA
264 km

KARANGAHAKE
GORGE

Waikino

THAMES

54 km

COROMANDEL ◄ 28 km ► COLVILLE

100 km

46 km

WHITIANGA ◄ 32 km ► COROMANDEL
via 309 ROAD

26 km

WHENUAKITE

31 km

HIKUAI ◄ 30 km ► THAMES
via INLAND ROAD

164 km

24 km

WHANGAMATA

29 km

WAIHI

54 km

TAURANGA

THAMES

HAMILTON

0   10   20

N

Kilometres

Coromandel Peninsula SH 25, 25a
Circuit 264 km

Coromandel is one of the North Island's top holiday destinations. Sheltered bays, beaches and harbours, the Coromandel Range, a thriving arts and crafts community and alternative lifestylers, and a long Maori and European history are among its attractions. Whilst the summer weather is usually good, Coromandel is prone to 'weather bombs' or just plain bad weather. Slips and road washouts are not uncommon, so it pays to contact information centres to check road conditions before setting out.

Thames–Coromandel SH 25
54 km, 1 hour

Thames – campground, walks

Thames' attractions include its museum (which recounts gold rush and logging eras) and the mineral displays at the mining school. Those interested in arts and crafts can purchase a guide to Coromandel's galleries at the Thames Information Centre. East of Thames in the Kauaeranga Valley (14 km) is a DoC visitor centre, a base for camping, walks and information about recreational activities in the Coromandel Range. A working kauri dam is a highlight. There are scrummy home-made chocolates to be bought at the Chocolate Shoppe, while the Twin Souls Café on Pollen Street at the northern end of the town is recommended. A boardwalk through mangroves to a Forest and Bird Protection Society bird hide begins near the Goldfields shopping complex and model railway.

Coromandel

Lined with pohutukawa, the road up the Thames coast to Coromandel is a lovely drive past mangrove-fringed bays, beaches, small settlements and craft galleries. Te Puru boasts an excellent little Thai café/take out, while at Waiomu the Coast to Kauri track (allow up to 3 hours return, brochure available) offers an easy walk from the coast past mining relics and regenerating forest to a magnificent stand of kauri. At Tapu (19 km from Thames), the diversion to the Rapaura Watergardens (6.5 km along the Tapu–Coroglen Road) is highly recommended. From Kereta, the road to Coromandel climbs to points overlooking Manaia and Coromandel harbours and the Hauraki Gulf. Stalls selling fresh mussels and oysters are found as the road rounds flats on the edge of Coromandel Harbour.

Coromandel's charm lies in the atmosphere conjured by its numerous sidewalk cafés, galleries and historic buildings dating from the gold rushes of the 1850s and 60s. The mining school has working models of quartz-crushing machinery and other nineteenth-century mining relics. Gold was struck for the first time in New Zealand at Driving Creek, a few kilometres north of Coromandel. These days Driving Creek is a haven for artisans and location of the famous narrow-gauge Driving Creek railway. Driving Creek also features potteries, working steam engines, a brickworks and café. Ten minutes past Driving Creek up Kennedy Bay Road (steep and unsealed) is the Tokatea Lookout and walk – a superb viewpoint. Café recommendations: Umu (for coffee and seafood) and Driving Creek Café for its relaxed garden setting, vegetarian food and a delectable selection of cakes. I was impressed too with The Source, a cooperative venture featuring the work of nine Coromandel craft artists located on Coromandel's main street.

Colville

Thirty minutes (28 km) north of Coromandel is this friendly village that launched the region's reputation for alternative lifestyles. The Colville Caff is reason alone to visit. Before Colville there are serviced campgrounds at Shelly, Long and Amodeo Bays and at Papaaroha. Legstretcher: The 40-minute coastal forest walk at Papaaroha.

Cape Colville – campground, walks

Many make the scenic drive (unsealed) north around the Moehau Range to Cape Colville/Port Jackson (29 km, 1 hour). However the road is rough. There are DoC campgrounds at Fantail Bay (18 km from Colville) and at Fletcher Bay, five minutes from Port Jackson.

Coromandel–Whitianga SH 25
46 km, 1 hour

Allow 1 hour for the pleasant drive along SH 25 which crosses the Coromandel Range to Whangapoua Harbour and Kuaotunu settlement (petrol, dairy, pleasant beaches and a campground nearby). Then it's a 16 km drive through another fragment of Coromandel Forest Park to Mercury Bay and Whitianga.

Coromandel–Whitianga via the '309 Road'
32 km, 50 minutes

An unsealed scenic route across the Coromandel Range, which begins off SH 25 about 4 km south of Coromandel. Highly recommended by the locals, this is nonetheless a rather narrow and winding drive. Apart from forest scenery, the highlights are the Waiau Waterworks (an eccentric and fun public garden) 9 km from Coromandel, Waiau Falls (popular swimming hole) and the nearby Kauri Grove (12 km, one of the few remaining unlogged kauri stands in the region: allow 30 minutes to walk through here on an easy path).

Whitianga–Waihi
75 km, 2 hours

Whitianga – campground, swimming, fishing

Once a major colonial port supporting the trade in kauri and kauri gum, Whitianga is now a rural service town and holiday resort. In summer tourists and holidaymakers gather to enjoy the area's beaches, water activities and coastal scenery. Of the cafés, Nina's and Coghill House are recommended here. You can take the passenger ferry for a quick crossing to Ferry Landing and walking access to Cooks Beach.

Hahei & Cooks Beach – campground, walks, swimming

Two of the Whitianga area's most popular locations. Hahei is 37 km from Whitianga (turnoff at Whenuakite) and its attractions include its beach, the Te Whanganui-A-Hei Marine Reserve and the Cathedral Cove walkway – an excellent interpreted coastal walk (2 hours return) with spectacular scenery. Luna

Café in the village makes great coffee. At Hot Water Beach, south of Hahei you can dig out your own natural spa on the beach two hours either side of low tide.

To reach Cooks Beach turn left on Purangi Road 2 km from the Whenuakite intersection. Cooks Beach is another sublime safe swimming area, and where Captain Cook and his astronomer observed the transit of Mercury across the sun in 1769. The Shakespeare Cliff walk offers panoramic views of Mercury Bay. It's a short drive from here to Flaxmill Bay (Eggscentric Café) and Ferry Landing (Tri Kiwi Café and art gallery) opposite Whitianga.

Tairua/Pauanui – campground, walk, swimming

Tairua (37 km from Whitianga) is an idyllic settlement near the mouth of Tairua Harbour. Out of the Blue café has a good reputation, offering vegetarian food as well as meatier options. Across the harbour (29 km by road), is the exclusive, purpose-built holiday-town of Pauanui. There is a good surf beach here and a rewarding though steep climb up Pauanui Mountain from the south end of Pauanui beach.

At Hikuai, 11 km from Tairua, you can return to Thames (30 km) via SH 25a, which wriggles through the Coromandel Range with excellent views of the Pinnacles along the way. Between Hikuai and Whangamata, side roads lead to Opoutere and Onemana beaches. Opoutere is halfway round mangrove-lined Wharekawa Harbour which has a great youth hostel and campground on its shores. Walks in dunelands and to the wildlife reserve (birdwatching) in the harbour estuary are recommended here. Onemana, more developed, has a lovely beach, views to the Alderman Islands, and Café Onemana.

Whangamata – campground, swimming

Whangamata's 3.8 km Ocean Beach has a renowned surf break. Like Whitianga, the population swells in summer and cafés and restaurants have emerged to meet the demand for good food and beverages. Try Vibes Café for a strong coffee with breakfast.

Waihi – campground, walks, swimming

After Whiritoa Beach, SH 25 climbs a hill and descends to Waihi, a modern goldmining town and holiday destination (29 km from Whangamata). Waihi trades on its long mining history with historic walks, relics, museum and vintage railway. If you've never visited an opencast mine, this is the place. Waihi's 'heart of gold', the Martha Mine in the centre of the town, is open for tours, otherwise find the Moresby Ave lookout where interpretation panels would have you believe that ripping open a 300 m deep hole is a most natural and environmentally sensitive activity.

Waihi–Thames via Paeroa
54 km, 1 hour

The highlights of this drive are the Waikino historic mining ruins and the scenic drive through Karangahake Gorge. Among Waikino's attractions are what's left of the largest quartz-crushing battery in Australasia, a visitor centre, museum, railway and tram rides and the Waikino Station Café. The Karangahake Gorge Historic Walkway takes in many of the ruins in this area. Waikino is also the centre of an established arts and crafts community. The gorge has picnic sites and safe swimming in the Ohinemuri River.

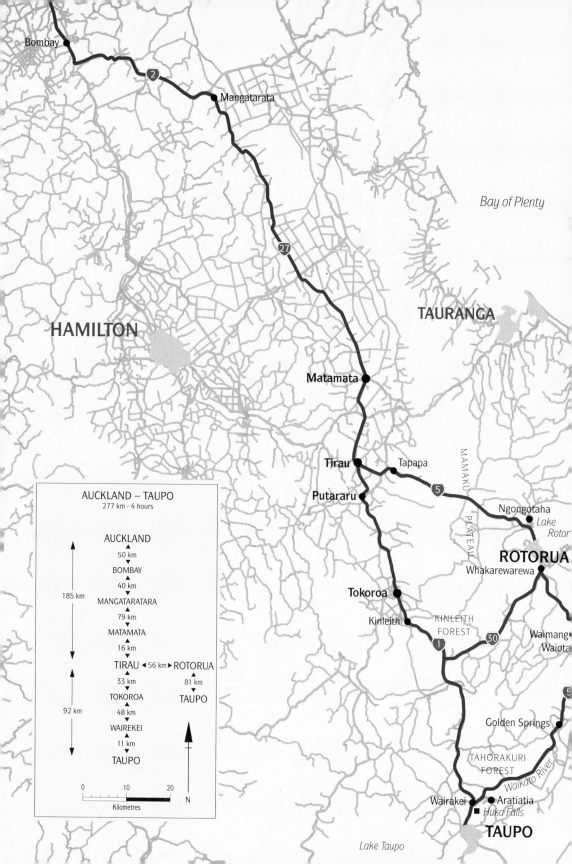

Bombay

(2)

Mangatarata

Bay of Plenty

(27)

TAURANGA

HAMILTON

Matamata

Tirau   Tapapa

(5)

MAMAKU

Putaruru

Ngongotaha
● *Lake
Rotor*

PLATEAU

ROTORUA

Whakarewarewa

Tokoroa

KINLEITH
FOREST

(30)

Kinleith

(1)

Waimang
Waiota

TAHORAKURI
FOREST

Golden Springs

Waikato River

Wairakei   ● Aratiatia
             ■ *Huka Falls*

TAUPO

Lake Taupo

AUCKLAND – TAUPO
277 km - 4 hours

AUCKLAND
▲
50 km
BOMBAY
▲
40 km
185 km   MANGATARATARA
▲
79 km
MATAMATA
▲
16 km
TIRAU ◄ 56 km ► ROTORUA
▲
33 km   81 km
TOKOROA   ▼
▲   TAUPO
48 km
92 km   WAIREKEI
▲
11 km
▼
TAUPO

0   10   20
|————|————|————|————|
Kilometres   N ▲

Auckland–Rotorua SH 1, 2, 27, 5
241 km, 3.5 hours

The fastest route to Rotorua from Auckland is the route via SH 1, 2, 27 and 5. Travelling from Auckland down SH 1, turn onto SH 2 south of Bombay and follow it through Mangatawhiri and Maramarua to Mangatarata (see Route 9 for other details on this leg). At Mangatarata take SH 27 and keep going through Matamata to Tirau.

Matamata
Workmans Café on Matamata's main street is the best café between Auckland and Rotorua. Tours of Hobbiton village built for Peter Jackson's film Lord Of The Rings is the town's most popular tourist activity these days. Book at the information centre.

Tirau
Tirau has a novel information centre and adjacent gallery promoting woolly things, and several good cafés (try Chuzzlewit or Alley Cats).

Just south of Tirau turn east onto SH 5 to Rotorua. From Tapapa SH 5 climbs onto the forested Mamaku Plateau – lovely driving through forest and volcanic landscapes to Ngongotaha on the shores of Lake Rotorua, 7 km from the Rotorua city centre.

Auckland–Taupo SH 2, 27, 1
277 km, 4 hours

Follow the route above to Tirau where SH 27 rejoins SH 1. From Tirau it's a straight run down SH 1 through Putararu, the mill towns of Tokoroa and Kinleith and long avenues of pine plantations in Kinleith Forest. (Allow 40 minutes to reach Rotorua via SH 30, which intersects 19 km from Tokoroa.) Tokoroa's Scoffers Café on Roseberry Street (one block from the information centre) is a foodie's oasis where you'll get good coffee as well. Five kilometres south of Wairakei is the turnoff to the spectacular Huka Falls, which is reached after a short easy walk.

Taupo – campground, water activities, walks
Idyllically situated, Taupo is world-renowned as the base for trout fishing on the lake and its tributary rivers. Cafés and bars abound, along with opportunities for fine dining, swimming, adventure sports and more sedate activities like a walk through the gardens of the Waipahihi Botanical Reserve. Lake Taupo's waters fill the crater formed by what's believed to be one of the world's largest volcanic eruptions.

Rotorua–Taupo SH 2, 27, 1
81 km, 1.5 hours

This route skirts the western edge of Kaingaroa Forest and takes in the major geothermal attractions at Whakarewarewa (3 km from Rotorua), Waimangu (25 km) and Waiotapu (30 km). Golden Springs (43 km) has a motorcamp and thermal baths. Beyond here much of the drive to Wairakei travels between the broad forested avenues formed by the Tahorakuri exotic forest. From Wairakei it's 11 km to Taupo. (See above).

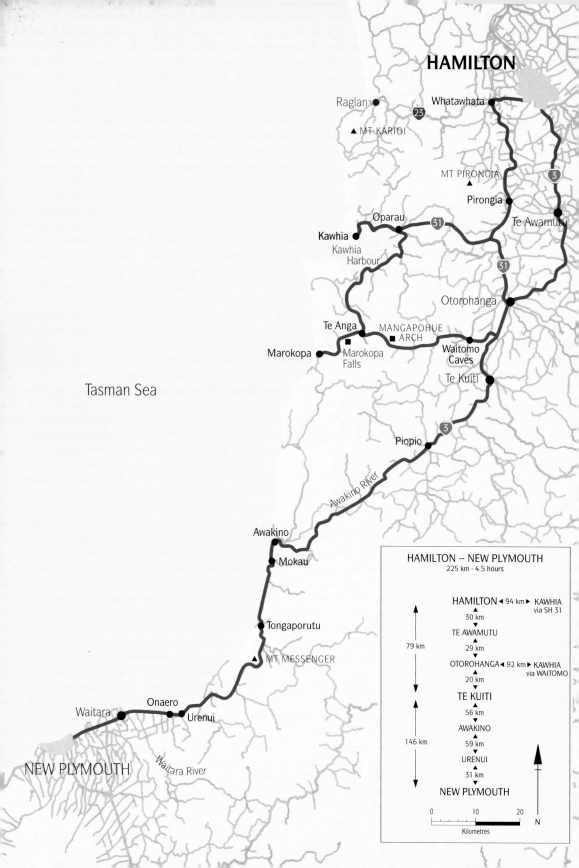

HAMILTON

Raglan
▲ MT KARIOI

⑳ 23

Whatawhata

③ 3

▲ MT PIRONGIA

Pirongia

Te Awamutu

Oparau

㉛ 31

Kawhia

Kawhia
Harbour

㉛ 31

Otorohanga

Te Anga

MANGAPOHUE
■ ARCH

Marokopa

■ Marokopa
Falls

Waitomo
Caves

Te Kuiti

③ 3

Piopio

Tasman Sea

Awakino River

Awakino

Mokau

Tongaporutu

▲ MT MESSENGER

Waitara

Onaero

Urenui

NEW PLYMOUTH

Waitara River

HAMILTON – NEW PLYMOUTH
225 km · 4.5 hours

	HAMILTON ◄ 94 km ► KAWHIA via SH 31	
	30 km ▼	
	TE AWAMUTU	
79 km	29 km ▼	
	OTOROHANGA ◄ 92 km ► KAWHIA via WAITOMO	
	20 km ▼	
	TE KUITI	
	56 km ▼	
	AWAKINO	
146 km	59 km ▼	
	URENUI	
	31 km ▼	
	NEW PLYMOUTH	

0   10   20
Kilometres

N

Hamilton–Kawhia SH 23, 31

94 km, 1 hour

The most straightforward way to Kawhia Harbour is to take SH 23 and turn south at Whatawhata towards Pirongia (SH 39). A good road past Pirongia leads to the SH 31 junction (from Otorohanga) which is then followed to the coast.

Kawhia – campground, swimming, fishing

Kawhia is not as flashy as Raglan but is no less charming and possesses a strong sense of its Maori and European history. Kawhia's museum is worth visiting. The drive to Ocean Beach offers views across the harbour and towards Mts Pirongia and Karioi, but the highlight is the hot pools that can be dug out of the sand at low tide. Annie's Café offers a respite from the area's otherwise relentless fish and chip culture. The 'back route' between Kawhia and Waitomo (1.5 hours, sealed) offers fine views and forests as it rounds Kawhia Harbour.

Hamilton–New Plymouth SH 3

225 km, 4.5 hours

I recommend locating (at visitor centres) the free *The Best of the West* heritage trail brochure, one of the better ones of its type, for its useful guide to this region.

Otorohanga

South of Hamilton SH 3 traverses dairying and sheep farming country in the Waipa Basin to Te Awamutu (Zest Café on Alexandra Street), then continues to Otorohanga. North Island brown kiwi and other native birds can be viewed at Otorohanga's Kiwi House.

Waitomo environs – campground, walks

Eight kilometres south of Otorohanga is the turnoff to Waitomo Caves where a range of underground adventures from easy to desperate can be arranged. As well as cave tours, there are several excellent short walks offering an above-ground perspective of Waitomo's limestone landsapes – get hold of DoC's *West to Marakopa* brochure from information centres. Highly recommended of these are walks to the Ruakuri Natural Tunnel, Marokopa Falls and the magnificent Mangapohue limestone arch. There is a campground, store and excellent beach at Marokopa, 1 hour from Waitomo.

Te Kuiti

Bosco's Café at the northern end of Te Kuiti has won awards and is priced to suit. A good place to stop nonetheless.

Mokau – campground, swimming, fishing

From Te Kuiti, SH 3 turns southwest. After Piopio the road winds through the Awakino Gorge to reach the coast at Awakino and shortly afterwards, the popular resort of Mokau (where you'll get good food and coffee at the River Run Café). Twenty minutes south of Mokau at Tongaporutu is the turnoff to the exhilarating White Cliffs Walkway – but get the DoC brochure available at visitor centres for an explanation of what's what before you go.

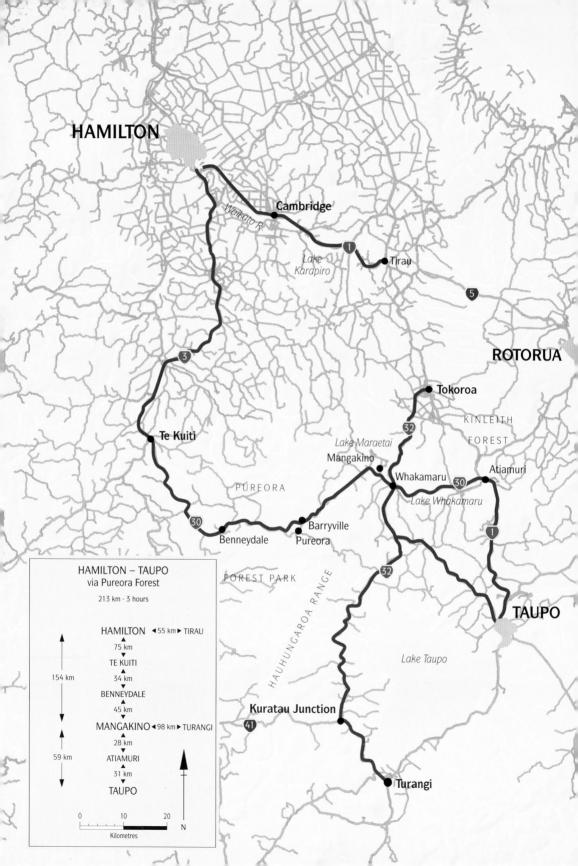

HAMILTON

Cambridge

Waikato R.

Lake Karapiro

①

Tirau

⑤

ROTORUA

③

●**Tokoroa**

KINLEITH

FOREST

Lake Maraetai

Mangakino

③②

Whakamaru

③⓪

Atiamuri

Lake Whakamaru

Te Kuiti

PUREORA

①

③⓪

●**Barryville**

Benneydale   **Pureora**

FOREST PARK

③②

TAUPO

HAUHUNGAROA RANGE

Lake Taupo

Kuratau Junction

④①

Turangi

HAMILTON – TAUPO
via Pureora Forest

213 km - 3 hours

HAMILTON ◄ 55 km ► TIRAU

75 km

TE KUITI

34 km

BENNEYDALE

45 km

MANGAKINO ◄ 98 km ► TURANGI

28 km

ATIAMURI

31 km

TAUPO

154 km

59 km

0   10   20

Kilometres

N

Urenui – campground, swimming, fishing

Between Tongaporutu and Urenui the highway climbs forested Mt Messenger. Back on coastal plains, Urenui is a popular holiday spot, locality for craft artists and the White Cliffs Brewery.

Hamilton–Tirau SH 1
55 km, 40 minutes

Pleasant countryside, busy road, but a useful connecting route to Rotorua and Taupo with the added bonus of being able to stop in Cambridge.

Cambridge

A leafy country town on the Waikato River with fine period buildings, antique shops, craft galleries, tree-lined streets, gardens, parks and a large free-flight aviary. The All Saints Café at the Cambridge Country Store is highly regarded among fine diners, but the superb Rata Café on Queen Street is my recommendation. The Boatshed Café at Lake Karapiro 10 km from Cambridge (follow signs from SH 1 down Gorton Road) is another worthwhile place to stop where you can rent kayaks or go on a guided trip on the lake.

See Route 11 for information on Tirau and beyond.

Hamilton–Taupo via Pureora Forest SH 3, 30, 1
213 km, 3 hours

The highlight of this drive is the 78,000 ha Pureora Forest Park, a remnant of a vast podocarp forest that dominated the area before it was logged.

Drive to Te Kuiti via SH 3 (1.25 hours, see Hamilton–New Plymouth, Route 15). From Te Kuiti, turn onto SH 30 which enters the hilly sheep-farming country west of Benneydale village (store, hotel, petrol). East of Benneydale the road passes briefly through the small forested Herekawa Scenic Reserve then reaches Maraeroa Road to Pureora after 20 minutes.

Pureora – campground, walks

Follow the gravel road to the Pureora visitor centre, located, ironically perhaps, in a fragment of native forest inside a plantation forest. The ultimately successful battle to save what was left of the tall trees of Pureora was one of the defining moments in New Zealand's conservation history. Two short walks I would recommend are the Totara Walk and the excellent Forest Tower Walk. Totara Walk (close to the centre) is an easy 30-minute loop amongst the enormous trees the area is known for. A self-guide brochure for tree identification is available. The Forest Tower Walk is signposted from Barryville Road (which returns to SH 30 east of Maraeroa Road). A short walk leads to the 12 m multilevel forest tower which allows you to climb into the forest canopy. Interpretation panels in the tower identify birds and trees.

Mangakino – campground

A settlement with friendly locals on the banks of Lake Maraetai and on the edge of Kinleith Forest. To reach Taupo, continue along SH 30 beside the Waikato River to the SH 1 junction before Atiamuri.

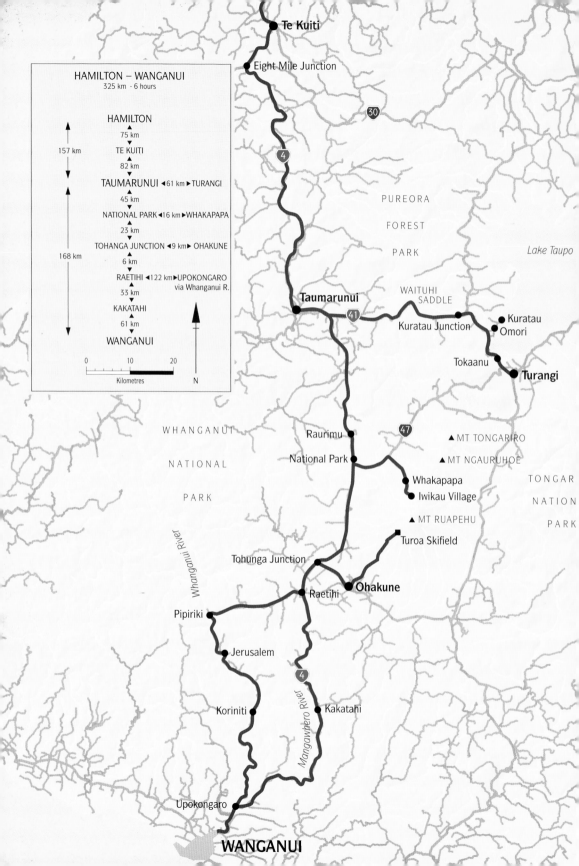

SH 30 meets SH 32 at Whakamaru (café). SH 32 links Tokoroa and Turangi between the western shores of Lake Taupo and the eastern flanks of the Pureora Forest. From this junction allow half an hour to reach Tokoroa or 1 hour to the junction with SH 41 at Kuratau and a further half-hour to Turangi. You can continue on SH 30 to SH 1, but a more direct route to Taupo from Whakamaru is to drive south on SH 32 for approximately 15 km then take the signposted route east to Taupo.

Hamilton–Wanganui SH 4
325 km, 6 hours

Take SH 3 to Te Kuiti (see Hamilton–New Plymouth, Route 15). SH 4 begins 11 km south of Te Kuiti at Eight Mile Junction and proceeds through the hilly mudstone and limestone hinterland between central North Island and eastern Taranaki. The road to Taumarunui is fairly windy though always scenic (1 hour).

Taumarunui

Maori have lived on the banks of the upper Whanganui River for centuries, using the river as the major route to the coast at Wanganui. The area was virtually off limits to Europeans until the 1880s. After Europeans settled here, and before road and rail, the river remained an important supply route to Taumarunui, while the journey by paddle steamer from Wanganui became one of the country's top tourist attractions. What now takes two hours by road was a three-day journey downstream by tourist paddle steamer. Easy canoeing trips on the river into Whanganui National Park remain a popular tourist activity. Among the dreary chip shops and tearooms on the main street you'll be pleased to find the fine Rivers II Café.

National Park – campground, walks

National Park settlement is just 25 minutes from Taumarunui. In this short time the landscape is transformed as it climbs from the enclosing hills of Taumarunui to the open tussock-covered plateau below Tongariro National Park's active volcanoes. Shortly before National Park, railway buffs will appreciate the Raurimu

Mt Ngaruhoe from Mt Tongariro, Tongariro National Park

Spiral lookout at Raurimu, though even the cartographically literate will struggle to decipher the explanatory map. National Park, at the junction with SH 47 to Turangi (49 km), offers ski lodges, cafés, bars and a myriad of purchasable adventures. The Station Café (next to the railway station) serves a better coffee than you'll get at Whakapapa village, 16 km from here in Tongariro National Park.

Whakapapa – campground, walks, skiing

Whakapapa's park visitor centre has excellent interpretive displays covering geology, flora and fauna, and the Maori and European relationships with this landscape – now a World Heritage Area. Walking options range from 15 minutes to all day. Most renowned is the day-long crossing of Mt Tongariro. The 6 km sealed road to Iwikau Village and skifield takes you into a raw landscape of lava flows, boulder fields, tussocks, impressive vistas and summertime chairlift rides.

The Grand Chateau at Whakapapa, Mt Ruapehu

Ohakune – campground, walks

If it's at all possible let the sun coat the western slopes of the volcanoes in the late afternoon or evening before you drive toward Ohakune. The vistas are magnificent. Turn off SH 4 at Tohunga Junction to reach Ohakune. In winter, Ohakune's nightclubs and bars are jammed with partying skiers. It's a quieter town in summer, but there are still several cafés open (Utopia is the pick of them). The 17 km drive (sealed) to Turoa skifield offers forest and alpine walks, picnicking and fine views. A park visitor centre is located at the park entrance a short distance from the town

Raetihi

Raetihi's main attraction is its proximity to Tongariro and Whanganui national parks. Whanganui National Park is 30 minutes west of SH 4 at Pipiriki (the last kilometres to Pipiriki are unsealed). Raetihi at least has a good café – Clowns – at the west end of the main shopping centre on the road to Pipiriki.

Pipiriki (Whanganui National Park) – walks, picnicking, boating

Pipiriki is where most kayakers and canoeists from Taumarunui finish their journey. There's a 30-minute walk from the DoC office, though the easiest way to experience the park is by jetboat – tours can be arranged here. Colonial House, a registered historic place, doubles as an information centre. Having come this far I'd recommend the river road down the Whanganui River to Wanganui (1.5-2 hours, covered by a heritage trail brochure). It's a slow, scenic journey, steeped in Maori and European history, with river and forest landscapes, pa, marae and sacred Maori sites. Such was the spiritual and practical relationship Maori had with the river, they named virtually every corner. Jerusalem, 11 km from Pipiriki, is most commonly associated with the commune established there by the revered poet James K Baxter. The beautiful Church of Hiruharama (Jerusalem), built in 1892, features a carved altar of Maori design, kowhaiwhai panels on its walls, and historical information about this remote community. The 31 km unsealed section to Koriniti is suitable for campervans. There are no shops or service stations until Upokongaro back on SH 4.

Raetihi–Wanganui

Allow 1.5 hours for the 94 km run to Wanganui on SH 4. The road is hilly and windy, traversing farmed land above the Mangawhero River much of the way. Fuel and refreshments are available at Kakatahi (33 km from Raetihi). A worth-while diversion is to drive 3–4 km up the Whanganui river road (42 km from Kakatahi) to a highpoint overlooking the Whanganui Valley at the beginning of Aramoana Walkway.

Taumarunui–Turangi SH 41
61 km, 40 minutes

This route crosses the forested Waihaha Scenic Reserve south of Pureora Forest Park. Waituhi Lookout on the crest of the range offers excellent views across Lake Taupo and the Tongariro volcanoes. After Kuratau Junction (43 km from Taumarunui), pleasant reserves and beaches at Omori and Kuratau on the shores of Lake Taupo are a short distance off the highway. Allow time to stop at the Tokaanu hot springs, a DoC facility where you can enjoy a pleasant soak and forest walks.

Canoes on the Whanganui River

TAUMARUNUI – STRATFORD
156 km (13 km unsealed) · 3 hours

TAUMARUNUI
▲
▼ 83 km
TAHORA
▲
▼ 17 km
WHANGAMOMONA
▲
▼ 38 km
DOUGLAS
▲
▼ 18 km
STRATFORD

N

0   10   20
Kilometres

Tangarakau River

Taumarunui

4

43

41

PAPARATA SADDLE

TANGARAKAU GORGE

Tahora

TAHORA SADDLE

NEW PLYMOUTH

Whangamomona

POHOKURA SADDLE

WHANGAMOMONA
SADDLE

Pohokura

National Park

Stratford

Douglas

Toko

Ohakune

WANGANUI

Taumarunui–Stratford SH 43
156 km (13 km unsealed), 3 hours

Called the Lost World Highway by tourism marketeers, this under-rated scenic drive into the hilly backblocks of eastern Taranaki traverses three saddles, forest reserves and the beautiful Tangarakau Gorge Scenic Reserve. The highway follows a sinuous path through the hills, but despite a 13 km unsealed section is still passable in a campervan.

SH 43 is a designated heritage trail and is supported with informative panels en route and a heritage trail brochure which points out walks and places of historical import. The history of the area is absorbing, encompassing Maori resistance to European settlement, coal mining, forest clearance and establishment of farms on marginal, slip-prone land, and the building of the road and railway through here. There is no petrol for 140 km (until Toko) so fuel up at Taumarunui.

The first scenic highlight is after the Ohinepa Scenic Reserve (toilets, camping, picnicking) at Nevins Lookout about 30 km from Taumarunui. After crossing Paparata Saddle the road reaches the still pools of the Tangarakau Gorge Scenic Reserve. On Tahora Saddle is the perfectly located Kaieto Café with fine views from the porch across forest remnants and farmed land slipping off the ridges to the Tongariro volcanoes. Such is the state of much of the land here you have to question the wisdom of those who cleared the forests believing the papa (mudstone) hills could sustain a monoculture. You can camp or park a campervan next to the café.

Whangamomona is the largest settlement on the route with its pub, backpackers and campground. From here SH 43 climbs to its high point, the 270 m Whangamomona Saddle. The final saddle, Pohokura, is just a few kilometres on, followed by the descent to easier travel east of Stratford.

Hill country near Taumarunui

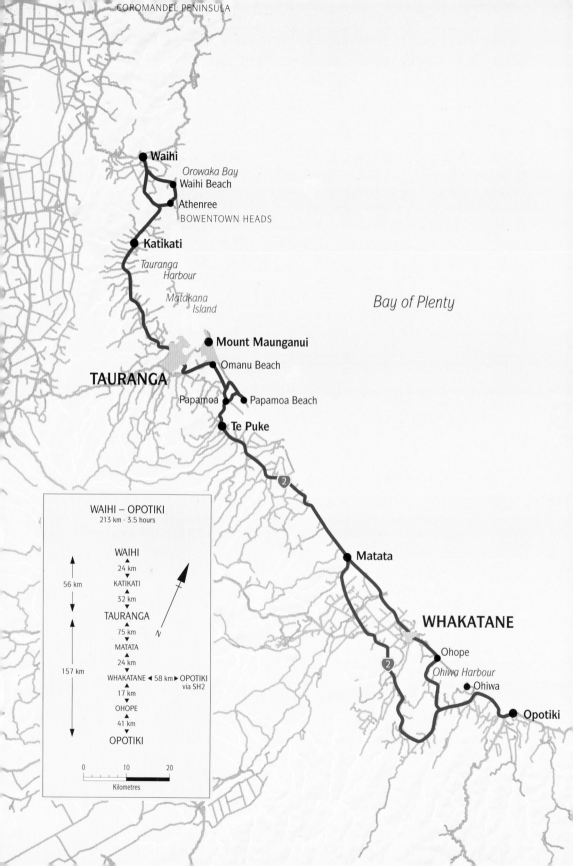

Waihi

Orowaka Bay
Waihi Beach

Athenree
BOWENTOWN HEADS

Katikati

*Tauranga
Harbour*

*Matakana
Island*

Bay of Plenty

Mount Maunganui

Omanu Beach

TAURANGA

Papamoa   Papamoa Beach

Te Puke

②

Matata

WHAKATANE

Ohope

Ohiwa Harbour

②   Ohiwa

Opotiki

WAIHI – OPOTIKI
213 km - 3.5 hours

56 km

157 km

WAIHI
▲
24 km
▼
KATIKATI
▲
32 km
▼
TAURANGA
▲
75 km
▼
MATATA
▲
24 km
▼
WHAKATANE ◀ 58 km ▶ OPOTIKI
via SH2
▲
17 km
▼
OHOPE
▲
41 km
▼
OPOTIKI

N

0   10   20
|‒‒‒‒‒‒‒‒‒‒‒‒‒‒‒‒‒‒‒|
Kilometres

Waihi–Opotiki SH 2
213 km, 3.5 hours

A drive through the hills and coastal plains of Bay of Plenty, passing Tauranga and resorts at Waihi Beach, Mount Maunganui and Ohope along the way. SH 2 is a busy road which services the region's market gardening, fruitgrowing and forestry industries.

Waihi Beach – campground, swimming
The turnoff to Waihi Beach is 4 km from Waihi. Waihi Beach occupies a lengthy sweep of coast south of Waihi. Between Waihi Beach settlement and the Bowentown Heads are safe swimming beaches, good surfing, hot pools at Athenree, camping, and a walk to Orokawa Bay at the north end of the beach.

Back on SH 2 the road skirts Tauranga Harbour through to Katikati, Tauranga and Mount Maunganui. Look for the Twickenham Café and gardens on the northern outskirts of Katikati which makes yummy cakes and excellent coffee. Wineries worth noting are Katikati's Morton Estate (winery and café), and Bethlehem's Mills Reef.

Mount Maunganui – campground, walks, swimming
Mount Maunganui (turn off SH 2 at Omanu Beach) has become a rather glitzy resort with any number of beachfront cafés. The beach is splendid while walks on the Mount offer outstanding coastal views over Tauranga Harbour, Matakana Island and the Bay of Plenty.

Papamoa Beach/Te Puke – campground, swimming
Papamoa Beach has a rapidly developing resort village and retirement haven, complete with shopping mall. On the beachfront is a nicely situated campground and the Blue Bijou café. Te Puke's Deli Café in the town centre is the pick of eating options here.

Whakatane/Ohope
From Te Puke the more scenic and quicker route to Opotiki is through Whakatane and Ohope and around Ohiwa Harbour. Te Puke to Whakatane takes 30 minutes (turn off SH 2 at Matata). Just past Ohope is the easy 1 hour walk around the Tauwhare Pa, a once fortified village, which overlooks Ohiwa Harbour. The pa has a fascinating history, and offers fine views and birdwatching. Café recommendations: The Bean (Strand East, Whakatane) and Café Surfside (Ohope).

Opotiki – campground, walks, swimming
Arching groves of pohutukawa enfold the highway as it nears Opotiki. A few minutes from the town on a roadside reserve are the arresting carved pou whenua Te Ara Ki Te Tairawhiti, the 'Pathway to the Sunrise' by artist Heke Collier, whose work is also found on Opotiki's main street. Those who require sustenance should try the excellent Two Fish café at 46 St John Street (on SH 35 virtually opposite the junction with SH 2) – the last place for a good coffee between here and Gisborne.

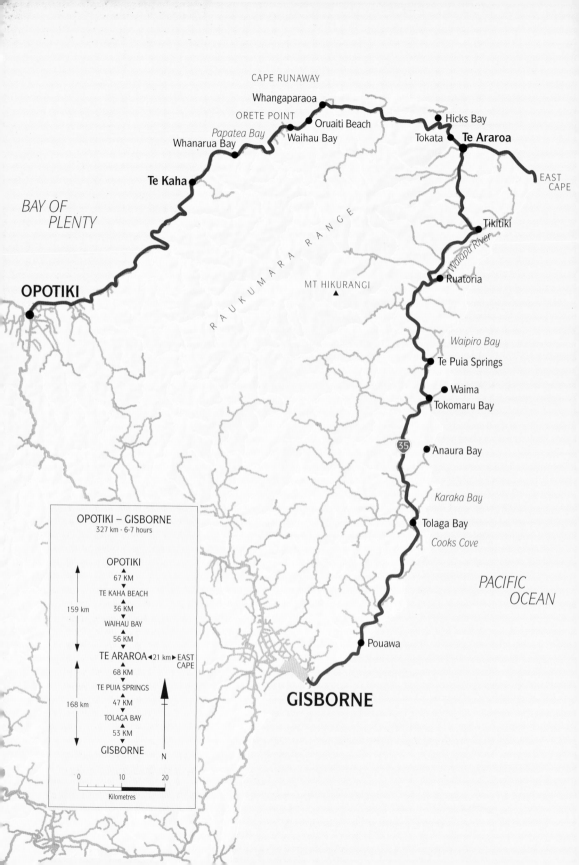

CAPE RUNAWAY

Whangaparaoa

ORETE POINT

Papatea Bay
Whanarua Bay

Oruaiti Beach

Waihau Bay

Hicks Bay

Tokata

Te Araroa

Te Kaha

EAST
CAPE

*BAY OF
PLENTY*

R A U K U M A R A   R A N G E

MT HIKURANGI ▲

Tikitiki

Waiapu River

Ruatoria

OPOTIKI

Waipiro Bay

Te Puia Springs

Waima

Tokomaru Bay

③⑤ Anaura Bay

Karaka Bay

Tolaga Bay

Cooks Cove

*PACIFIC
OCEAN*

Pouawa

GISBORNE

OPOTIKI – GISBORNE
327 km · 6-7 hours

OPOTIKI
▲ 67 KM
TE KAHA BEACH
▲ 36 KM
159 km   WAIHAU BAY
▼ 56 KM
TE ARAROA ◀21 km▶ EAST
CAPE
▲ 68 KM
TE PUIA SPRINGS
168 km   ▼ 47 KM
TOLAGA BAY
▼ 53 KM
GISBORNE

N

0   10   20

Kilometres

Opotiki–Gisborne SH 35
327 km, 6–7 hours

The drive around East Cape from Opotiki to Gisborne is one of the most memorable in New Zealand. Here, Maori communities have steadfastly maintained links with their culture, history and landscape. Evidence of this is everywhere in the numerous marae with their distinctive carved or painted wharenui (meeting houses), and in their memorials and schools. You can't just walk onto a marae – here and anywhere else in the country permission must be granted first and appropriate welcomes offered to visitors – not something organised lightly. But you never know, a chat with a friendly local can do wonders.

European history, particularly that associated with Captain James Cook, is another distinctive feature of the region. This history is recounted in numerous places: the Cook Landing Site National Historic Reserve in Gisborne, the wharf at Tolaga Bay, and the beautiful Tikitiki Church in which the melding of European and Maori culture is evocatively illustrated.

Most settlements have a store, but for the passing traveller petrol is expensive, tearoom food is produced from pie warmers and vats of fat, and no one has cracked the art of making a good coffee. The key to truly rewarding experiences on the Cape is to spend a night or two with locals like Paul and Maryanne of Te Kaha Lodge, which is likely to yield splendid kaimoana (seafood) and hospitality – kia ora!

Between Labour Weekend (last weekend in October) and Easter it is possible to freedom camp at Waipiro Bay, Tokomaru Bay, Kaiaua Beach, Tolaga Bay, Waihau Bay, Pouawa and Turihawa Beach.

Opotiki–Whangaparaoa 118 km
This first leg of SH 35 more or less hugs the Bay of Plenty coast as far as Whangaparaoa, in places cutting high onto bluffs and hills, allowing views of the spectacular land and seascape, and into the forested Raukumara hinterland. Beaches and campgrounds reinforce the holiday feel of this coastal section of the highway where there are numerous places to camp, swim, fish, snorkel, dive, picnic or go horse trekking.

Opape/Marenui Hill/Omaio – beaches, walks, camping
Opape is worth noting for the new Tauturangi Walkway (signposted, brochure available, 40 minutes to an hour return, great coastal views). Maraenui Hill 20 km from Opape offers a spectacular outlook before the road descends to cross the wide and beautiful Motu River. Free camping is allowed at the Omaio Reserve.

Te Kaha – campground, swimming, fishing
Once a whaling village, Te Kaha is these days a popular holiday destination with safe swimming and fishing, a store, splendid meeting house and what remains of a redoubt at Te Kaha Tukaki marae.

Whanarua Bay – campground, picnicking, swimming, fishing
Claimed to have its own microclimate, the bay's central attractions are its secluded beaches, swimming and fishing, and coastal views from Karirangi Hill including White Island. The Pacific Macadamia Nut Farm sells a range of macadamia products, and also runs a small café offering a healthier line of food

including panini and scrummy muffins.

Waihau Bay – campground, picnicking, swimming, fishing

Another popular destination with a store/tearooms where you can get a good breakfast fry-up. Nearby Oruaiti Beach is considered the best on this stretch. At Orete Point near the Waihau Bay Lodge (really just a flash pub) is a plaque commemorating the fact that in 1897 'nothing happened'.

Whangaparaoa

Steeped in Maori history, Whangaparaoa has a reinstated pa and meeting house open to visitors, while guided historic tours of the area over Maori land are also offered. The beach at Whangaparaoa Bay is said to be where the Tainui and Arawa canoes landed with their cargo of colonisers from Hawaiiki circa 1350 AD.

Whangaparaoa–Gisborne 209 km

South of Cape Runaway is the Ngati Porou tribal area. From Whangaparaoa, SH 35 remains inland for much of the route to Gisborne, the exceptions being sections from Hicks Bay to Te Araroa and Pouawa to Gisborne.

Hicks Bay

Hicks Bay occupies an important place in the history of the Ngati Porou, whose people have lived here for up to 1000 years. There are many historic sites and excavated fortifications. Tuwhakairiora meeting house, 'one of the finest in the East Cape', was named for a famous warrior to whom the area's original families trace their lineage. St Barnabas Church (1979) in the marae grounds is embellished with Maori art and exhibits a marriage of traditional and recent architecture.

Te Araroa

From Hicks Bay the road presents excellent views over the coast before the descent to the Tokata Flats where there is a holiday park. Soon after is the coastal settlement of Te Araroa. What is claimed to be the country's oldest (600 years) and largest pohutukawa (named Te Waha-o-Rerekohu) stands on the edge of Hinerupe marae on the beach front.

East Cape Lighthouse – walk

From Te Araroa you can drive to New Zealand's most easterly point and climb the several hundred steps to the East Cape lighthouse atop Otiki Hill (42 km return, mostly unsealed, 20 minutes one way. Watch out for wandering stock and horses). The track crosses Ngati Porou land, and although permission isn't required, a small koha (donation) is requested.

Tikitiki

Between Te Araroa and Tikitiki, SH 35 traverses rural and forest landscapes and climbs high onto a ridge offering views of the Raukumara Range and the Waiapu Mountains – the sacred peaks of the Ngati Porou – the highest and most important of these being Mt Hikurangi (1752 m). On a fine day Hikurangi can be seen from many places between Tikitiki and Te Puia.

Tikitiki on the north bank of the Waiapu River is where the beautiful St Mary's Church is located. Like Hicks Bay, excavated fortifications dating to the 1860 land wars are found on the hill above the settlement.

Ruatoria
Nineteen kilometres further is Ruatoria, East Cape's largest settlement which is dominated by views of Mt Hikurangi and nearby peaks. By late 2004 the owners of Ruatoria's What on Earth gift shop (worth a visit in its own right for local crafts) hope to have opened a café selling 'healthy food and good coffee' – for which there is most certainly a need on the East Cape!

South of Ruatoria, enquire at the Te Puia Springs Hotel about a dip in the hot springs.

Memorial Hall, Ruatoria

Tokomaru Bay – swimming
The welcoming sweep of Tokomaru Bay is reached 11 km from Te Puia. As well as catering for holiday-makers with a range of accommodation and services, Tokomaru Bay is a favoured haunt of fishers and local artists and crafts people. There is a safe beach, and the Te Puka Tavern on the road east towards Waima is just a few metres from the sea. There are four marae at the bay including Pakirikiri marae (1934) which has a large carved meeting house.

Anaura Bay – campground, walks
From Tokomaru Bay the road returns inland and climbs high through prime East Cape sheep farming country. Anaura Bay, a 7 km diversion from SH 35 about 22 km from Tokomaru Bay, has a campground and a 3.5 km coastal walkway through farmland and forest.

Tolaga Bay – walks
Tolaga Bay (36 km from Tokomaru Bay, 53 km from Gisborne) is renowned for the 700 metre concrete jetty at the bay's southern end. Completed in 1929, the jetty serviced coastal shipping until 1967. Though in need of restoration the jetty is still used by recreational fishers or those who want a stroll. Near the wharf is the Cooks Cove walkway (allow 2–3 hours) through farm and forest and along cliff tops to a lookout, the Hole in the Wall and Cooks Cove itself. A memorial records the visit of Captain Cook to Tolaga Bay in October 1769.

Pouawa–Gisborne
At Pouawa is the Te Tapuwae O Rongokako marine reserve which is administered by the Department of Conservation, local iwi, and recreational and commercial fishers. Pouawa is a popular free-camping, swimming and diving area, though fishing is banned in the reserve. The drive to Gisborne follows the Pacific coast through several small settle-ments and past formal and informal camping sites on the edge of surf and swimming beaches.

BAY OF PLENTY

OPOTIKI

Waioeka Pa

Okiore

Waioeka River

Wairata

Manganuku

②

Motu River

Motu

Matawai

Waihuka River

Otoko

Te Karaka

Ormond

GISBORNE

Poverty Bay

RAUKUMARA RANGE

HUIARAU RANGE

Lake Waikaremoana

OPOTIKI – GISBORNE
via the Waioeka Gorge
142 km - 2.5 hours

OPOTIKI
▲
▼ 70 km
MATAWAI ◄18 km► MOTU
▲
▼ 18 km
OTOKO
▲
▼ 23 km
TE KARAKA
▲
▼ 31 km
GISBORNE

N

0   10   20
Kilometres

Opotiki–Gisborne via the Waioeka Gorge SH 2
142 km, 2.5 hours

The highlight of this route is the 45 km Waioeka Gorge which begins 14 kilometres south of Opotiki.

Waioeka Gorge
At the entrance to the gorge is Waioeka River Kayak company offering easy 2 hour trips on the river. Into the gorge and following the Waioeka River, the road winds between the steep forested flanks of the Huiarau and Raukumara ranges. Three kilometres from the kayak operation is the Waioeka nature trail, a worthwhile and easy 15-minute interpreted forest walk.

Seven kilometres further is the start of the Tauranga Track where a short walk leads to a recently restored historic suspension bridge. The Manganuku campground (DoC), 47 km from Opotiki, has toilets and barbecue sites, and is the start of a couple of longer tramping routes.

Matawai – campground
After the campground the highway leaves the gorge and ascends Traffords Hill then crosses into the upper reaches of the Motu River to Matawai village. The 18 km diversion north from Matawai along a sealed road to Motu is of interest for those keen on horsetrekking, mountain-biking, walking, rafting and fishing. The easy Whinray Reserve Bush Walk to Motu Falls is recommended.

Te Karaka
Back on SH 2 the journey to Gisborne follows the Waihuka River, passing Otoko (where you can take a walk along the Otoko Walkway – all that remains of the old Moutohora railway link to Gisborne) and Te Karaka on the Poverty Bay river flats.

Motu River

Ormond
Towards Ormond you enter Gisborne's prosperous horticultural and wine-growing area. Along this stretch is the so-called 'slope of gold' chardonnay-growing area. A number of wineries are located hereabouts including Longbush, TW, Acton Estate and the Pouparae Park boutique winery. Wine tastings at these wineries are by appointment only. Montana's wines can be tasted at their shop on Lyttons Road in Gisborne. (See Gisborne–Wairoa, Route 23 for locations of other wineries.)

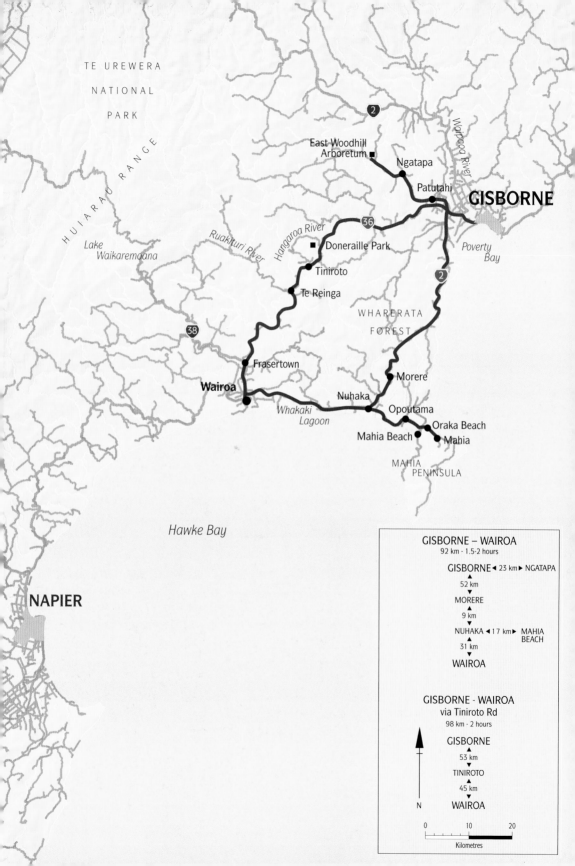

TE UREWERA

NATIONAL

PARK

HUIARAU RANGE

Lake
Waikaremoana

Ruakituri River

Hangaroa River

East Woodhill
Arboretum ■

Ngatapa

(2)

Waipaoa River

Patutahi

GISBORNE

(36)

■ Doneraille Park

Poverty
Bay

Tiniroto

Te Reinga

(2)

WHARERATA

FOREST

(38)

Frasertown

Morere

Wairoa

Nuhaka

Whakaki
Lagoon

Opoutama

Oraka Beach

Mahia Beach

Mahia

MAHIA
PENINSULA

Hawke Bay

NAPIER

GISBORNE – WAIROA
92 km - 1.5-2 hours

GISBORNE ◀ 23 km ▶ NGATAPA

▲
52 km
▼

MORERE

▲
9 km
▼

NUHAKA ◀ 17 km ▶ MAHIA
BEACH

▲
31 km
▼

WAIROA

GISBORNE - WAIROA
via Tiniroto Rd
98 km - 2 hours

GISBORNE

▲
53 km
▼

TINIROTO

▲
45 km
▼

WAIROA

N

0   10   20

Kilometres

Gisborne–Wairoa SH 2
92 km, 1.5–2 hours

From Gisborne SH 2 enters the Poverty Bay flats through the Matawhero winegrowing area, and heads south towards the large Wharerata pine plantation and Mahia Peninsula.

About 2 km towards Wairoa and Napier from the SH 2 turnoff to Opotiki is Riverpoint Road at the end of which is the Matawhero vineyard and the Colosseum Café. Just over the Waipaoa River a right turn at the roundabout onto Patutahi/Ngatapa Road leads to the Shalimar Estate vineyard. Highly recommended is to continue on this road past Ngatapa to the internationally renowned East Woodhill Arboretum (35 km from Gisborne, sealed road).

Morere – campground, walks
Morere hot springs 52 km from Gisborne at the south end of Wharerata forest is an attractively laid out spa in a 200 ha native forest reserve. As well as a variety of public and private thermal pools, the reserve has a number of forest walks. A great place for a pause.

Mahia Peninsula – campgrounds, walks, surfing, swimming
At Nuhaka is the turnoff to the Mahia Peninsula, a very popular surfing, swimming and holiday destination. Mahia Beach settlement is 17 km from Nuhaka at the south end of Opoutama Beach. The drive there is sealed and offers fine views along the peninsula, and is particularly dramatic in the evenings when a strong swell is running and low sun lights the clifflines. Beyond Mahia Beach the sealed road, now somewhat narrower, continues to Oraka Beach and Mahia on the peninsula's eastern side.

Back on SH 2 it's a straight run west past Whakaki lagoon into Wairoa.

Gisborne–Wairoa via Tiniroto SH 6 (The Tiniroto Road)
98 km, 1.5–2 hours

This alternative route to SH 2 winds through the hilly and often spectacular rural hinterland west of Gisborne. The road is sealed and narrow in places. Highlights include Doneraille Park (47 km from Gisborne), a forest reserve next to the Hangaroa River, with safe swimming, a campground and toilets. Three kilometres from Tiniroto is Hackfalls Arboretum which has a large collection of oaks, poplars and maples.

Te Reinga Falls is in one of the few scraps of native forest left in the area a short distance along Ruakituri Valley Road from Te Reinga. The impressive 18 m falls tumble over a sandstone bluff into a narrow slot which the nimble-footed can get a better view of from an informal track which descends to a rock platform. Slippery when wet! Frasertown (91 km from Gisborne, 7 km from Wairoa) is a small town at the junction with SH 38 which leads to Te Urewera National Park. (See Rotorua–Wairoa, Route 26).

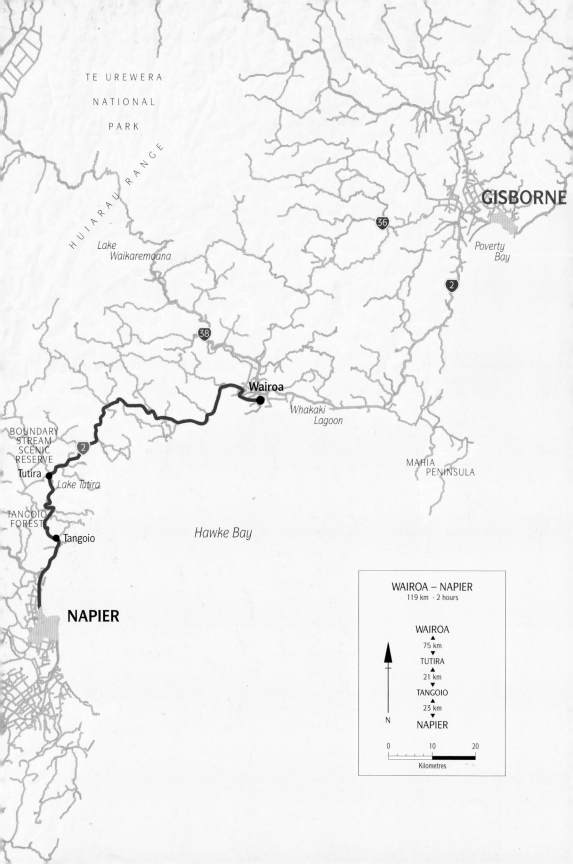

TE UREWERA

NATIONAL

PARK

HUIARAU RANGE

*Lake
Waikaremoana*

GISBORNE

*Poverty
Bay*

36

2

38

Wairoa

*Whakaki
Lagoon*

BOUNDARY
STREAM
SCENIC
RESERVE

2

Tutira

Lake Tutira

MAHIA
PENINSULA

TANGOIO
FOREST

Tangoio

Hawke Bay

NAPIER

WAIROA – NAPIER
119 km · 2 hours

WAIROA
▲
75 km
▼
TUTIRA
▲
21 km
▼
TANGOIO
▲
23 km
▼
NAPIER

N

0   10   20

Kilometres

Wairoa–Napier SH 2
119 km, 2 hours

This route traverses the hilly rural hinterland between Wairoa and Napier, passing several small settlements and high points with views toward Hawke Bay. Closer to Napier are several interesting reserves: Lake Tutira, White Pine Bush and Tangoio.

Lake Tutira – picnicking, swimming, walks, fishing

Seventy-five kilometres from Wairoa, the Lake Tutira wildlife refuge and its environs occupies a special place in New Zealand conservation history thanks to the efforts of a pioneer farmer and conservationist Herbert Guthrie Smith. A carpark at the southern end provides access to a pleasant picnic site and the start of several walking tracks.

Boundary Stream Scenic Reserve – walks

Boundary Stream, a 700 ha forest remnant north of Tutira (75 km from Wairoa) is one of six 'mainland islands' established by the Department of Conservation. The 'mainland island' concept involves a determined effort to reduce introduced pests such as rats, stoats and possums to enable native plants and animals to recover, and even allow the re-introduction of endangered species that might otherwise only survive on islands offshore. Although such islands involve a long range view, in just a few years there are encouraging signs that birdlife and forest species are staging a recovery at Boundary Stream. To reach the reserve, turn onto Matahorua Road by the Tutira store. For an interesting walk, take the lefthand fork (about 6 km from the store) onto Pohukura Road and drive to the Kamahi Loop track, a 2 hour loop through a varied lowland podocarp and kamahi forest.

White Pine Bush/ Tangoio Falls – picnicking, walks

A 19 ha forest remnant 96 km from Wairoa features tall kahikatea (white pine) and other rainforest trees that once covered the rest of the surrounding landscape. A 30-minute loop through the forest (best done anticlockwise) is accessible to wheelchairs. Two kilometres on is the Tangoio Falls Scenic Reserve where there is a 15-minute forest walk to Te Ana Falls.

Kahikatea trees

From here SH 2 winds through pine forest to reach the Hawke Bay coastline just past Tangoio settlement, 23 km from Napier.

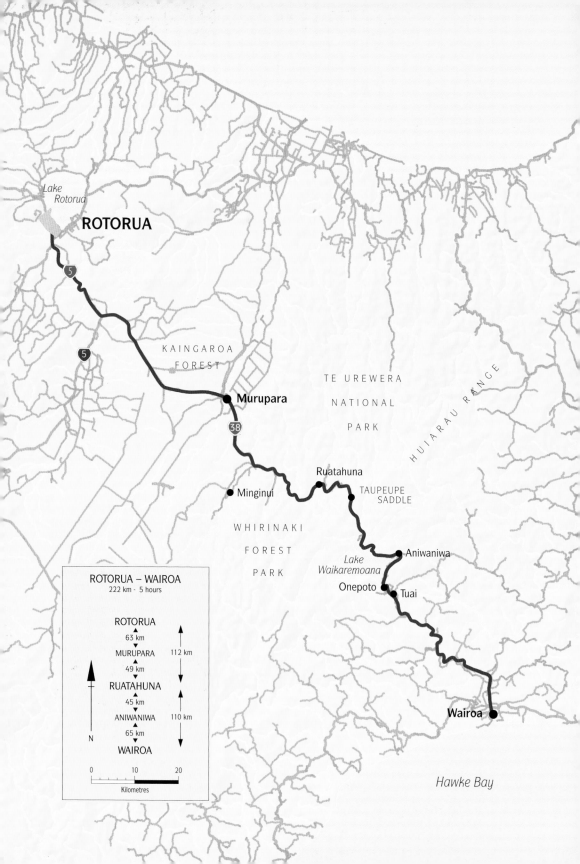

Lake Rotorua

ROTORUA

(5)

(5)

KAINGAROA
FOREST

Murupara

(38)

TE UREWERA

NATIONAL

PARK

Ruatahuna

HUIARAU RANGE

● Minginui

TAUPEUPE
SADDLE

WHIRINAKI

FOREST

PARK

Lake Waikaremoana

Aniwaniwa

Onepoto ● Tuai

Wairoa

Hawke Bay

ROTORUA – WAIROA
222 km · 5 hours

ROTORUA
▲
63 km
MURUPARA
▲
49 km
RUATAHUNA
▲
45 km
ANIWANIWA
▲
65 km
WAIROA

112 km

110 km

N

0   10   20
Kilometres

Rotorua–Waikaremoana–Wairoa
SH 5, 38 and 120 km of unsealed road
222 km, 5 hours

On the plus side, the road to Lake Waikaremoana ranks as one of the most scenic in this book, involving, by my estimation, the longest forest drive in New Zealand – the 102 km between Murupara and Onepoto at Lake Waikaremoana in Te Urewera National Park. The area is remote, covered in dense podocarp and beech forest, and resounds with Maori history and culture. On the negative, the route is mostly unsealed and often narrow, locals drive it too fast, and unfortunately some tourists can't handle the hazards. That said, by New Zealand standards of unsealed roads, it rates as one of the better ones for road surface. Campervans can make the journey, but check your insurance first (as should drivers of all rentals).

From Rotorua take SH 5 to the SH 38 junction (26 km) and proceed through Kaingaroa Forest to Murupara (1 hour).

Murupara

Visit the DoC office here for information on the road, camping sites, and walks. Allow 2 hours to reach Aniwaniwa (excluding sightseeing!) from Murupara. Beyond Murupara the road approaches the barrier of hills formed by the Te Urewera ranges, passing a sign indicating a winding road for a mere 120 km. The tarmac ends not far past the turnoff to Minginui and Whirinaki Forest Park (an outstanding podocarp reserve with a roadend campground and many rewarding forest walks).

Ruatahuna

A farming locality cleared from the forest, and traditional centre of the Tuhoe people who have inhabited the Te Urewera ranges for hundreds of years. Whole families on horseback driving stock is a diverting and not uncommon sight around these parts. From Ruatahuna the road climbs to Papiiora Ridge with fine views of ranges and forest. The road then crosses Taupeupe Saddle (919 m) on the crest of the Huiarau Range from where the rivers and the road drop toward the northern arm of Lake Waikaremoana.

Aniwaniwa Visitor Centre – campground, walks

The descent to and drive around the lake to Aniwaniwa is one of increasingly beautiful vistas. There are several roadside camping sites on this section. At Aniwaniwa, the national park information centre provides an absorbing interpretation of the natural and cultural values of this region. From the visitor centre the road continues along the eastern shore until the forest abruptly ends and the road descends steeply to Tuai. At Tuai is the incongruous Rangers Café and Bar (saddles on bar stools, yee-ha) with adjacent accommodation and campsites.

Beech forest, Te Urewera National Park

Allow 1 hour to Wairoa from Tuai.

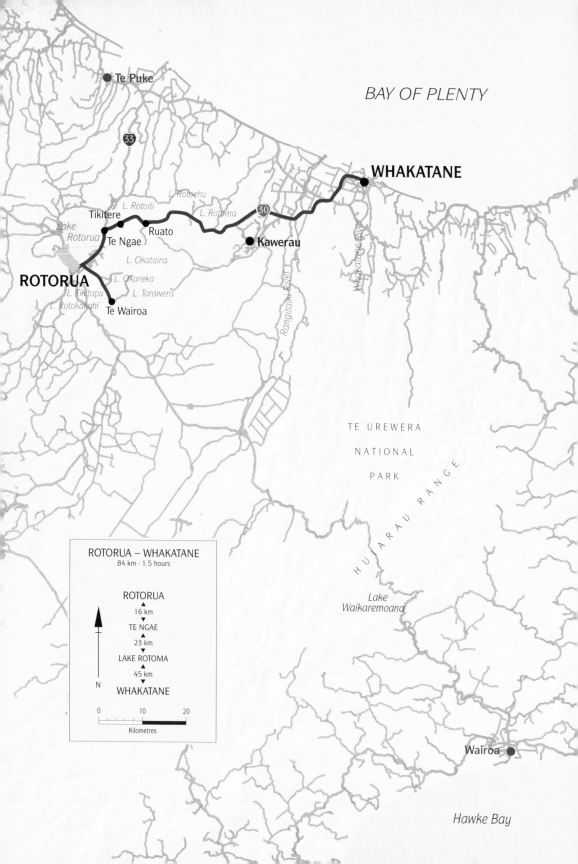

BAY OF PLENTY

● Te Puke

(33)

L. Rotoehu

L. Rotoiti

Tikitere

L. Rotoma

(30)

Ruato

Lake Rotorua

Te Ngae

● Kawerau

ROTORUA

L. Okataina

L. Okareka

L. Tikitapu

L. Tarawera

L. Rotokakahi

Te Wairoa

WHAKATANE

Whakatane River

Rangitaiki River

TE UREWERA

NATIONAL

PARK

HUIARAU RANGE

Lake
Waikaremoana

Wairoa ●

Hawke Bay

ROTORUA – WHAKATANE
84 km · 1.5 hours

ROTORUA
▲
16 km
▼
TE NGAE
▲
23 km
▼
LAKE ROTOMA
▲
45 km
▼
WHAKATANE

N

0   10   20
Kilometres

Rotorua–Whakatane SH 30
84 km, 1.5 hours

The string of beautiful lakes between Rotorua and Whakatane are the highlights of this drive. You could spend any amount of time swimming, picnicking, fishing, boating or walking at these lakes which also have high natural and cultural values.

Lakes Okareka, Tikitapu, Rotokakahi & Tarawera – campground, walks, water recreation
This sequence of lakes is reached by turning off SH 30 at Lynmore, 3 km from Rotorua by Whakarewarewa Forest Park. The lakes are well signposted and are reached along sealed roads. Lakes Tikitapu and Okareka are both 11 km from Rotorua. Tikitapu has a campground and store and at its southern end is a viewpoint which also overlooks Rotokakahi. Lake Okareka offers picnicking in a quiet reserve. The Te Wairoa buried village is reached shortly before Lake Tarawera after a pleasant forested drive. Here there is a café, museum and tours of the village.

Back on SH 30, the route skirts the eastern shores of Lake Rotorua then turns inland towards Lake Rotoiti. (SH 33 to Te Puke turns off at Te Ngae – allow 40 minutes.)

Tikitere (Hells Gate Thermal Reserve) – walks, picnicking
Not far from Te Ngae is this iwi-owned thermal reserve, the most active thermal area in the region. Rotorua's only mud volcano and the largest hot waterfall in this hemisphere are among its attractions.

Lakes Rotoiti, Rotoehu, Okataina & Rotoma – walks, picnicking, water recreation
A picnic area at the eastern end of Lake Rotoiti also has an easy track to the more secluded Lake Rotoehu. Halfway around Lake Rotoiti at Ruato is the turnoff to Lake Okataina, perhaps the prettiest of the lakes with its native forest surrounds. There are a number of short forest walks from the road end. There is a campground at Lake Rotoma.

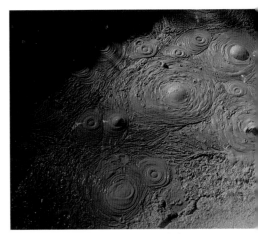

Mud pool, Tikitere

From Rotoma, SH 30 descends through native forests and pine plantations, past the loop road to Kawerau, and onto the Rangitaiki River plains to Whakatane.

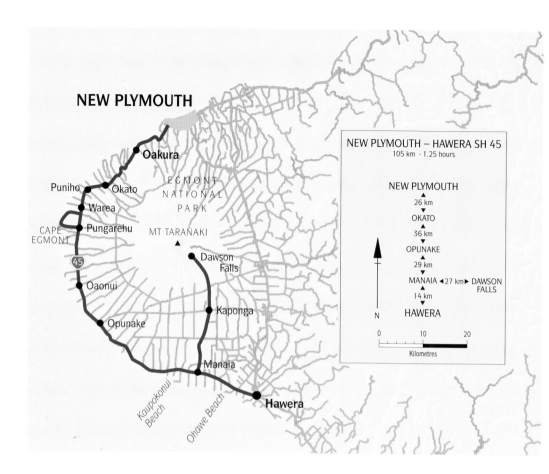

NEW PLYMOUTH – HAWERA SH 45
105 km - 1.25 hours

NEW PLYMOUTH
▲
26 km
▼
OKATO
▲
36 km
▼
OPUNAKE
▲
29 km
▼
MANAIA ◄27 km► DAWSON
▲   FALLS
14 km
▼
HAWERA

N

0   10   20

Kilometres

New Plymouth–Hawera via SH 45
105 km, 1.25 hours

The 'Surf Highway' is a great scenic drive around the western side of Mt Taranaki. Highlights are surfing and swimming beaches, Pukeiti Gardens, views of Mt Taranaki and Opunake's Sugar Juice Café.

Oakura – campground
Oakura, 15 km from New Plymouth, is Taranaki's most popular beach resort, with a family friendly beach, excellent swimming and surfing, picnic sites and patrolled swimming areas. The Green Ginger Café is the pick of the cafés here.

Pukeiti Gardens – walks
A few kilometres south of Oakura is the turnoff to Pukeiti Gardens (11 km from the highway up Upper Pitone Road), the internationally renowned rhododendron garden set amongst rainforest on the edge of Egmont National Park. The 360-hectare garden is one of the largest of its type in the world, and its

collection of rhododendrons is botanically very significant. Open all year, though October–November is best for rhododendron flowers.

Oakura–Opunake

Beaches beyond Oakura are wilder and more remote and are reached via side roads signposted as you drive through Okato, Puniho, Warea and Pungarehu. A right turn down Bayly Road (just past Warea) takes you to the coast and a loop back to SH 45 before Pungarehu. Parihaka Pa, site of the world's first passive resistance movement against colonial forces (said to have inspired Gandhi) is reached via Parihaka Road signposted ahead of Pungarehu (call 06 763 8708 to visit the pa). Sunset on Mt Taranaki viewed from Cape Egmont lighthouse, 6 km west of Pungarehu, is another highlight. The curious hillocks either side of the road are the congealed lahars (mudflows) from past eruptions of the omnipresent volcano to the east. At Oaonui is the Maui gas production factory, the onshore facility where gas piped ashore from the South Taranaki Bight is processed.

Opunake – campground, walks

Opunake's Middleton Bay features a clifftop walking track and lookout over the coast. There's a popular beachfront campground and safe swimming from the beach, while the Sugar Juice Café on the main street is the best of the region's travellers' cafés by a long margin.

Mt Taranaki from New Plymouth

Kaupokonui and Ohawe Beaches – swimming, beach walks

Both of these popular beaches (signposted before and after Manaia respectively) are worth the diversion off SH 45.

Dawson Falls – walks

Dawson Falls in Egmont National Park is 20 minutes by a good road from Manaia, past the Kapuni natural gas production facility, and Kaponga village (fuel). Dawson Falls has luxury and backpacker accommodation, a park visitor centre, and a number of short walks and longer excursions on the flanks of Mt Taranaki. Recommended short walks are those to Wilkies Pools and to Dawson Falls.

Hawera

Distinguished by its impressive 1914 water tower, Hawera has many other notable historic buildings (a self-guide brochure on these is available from the visitor centre below the tower), and the widely acclaimed Tawhiti Museum (signposted from the centre of town) – considered one of the country's best private museums (café). One of the museum's displays is a re-creation of the huge Turuturu Mokai pa, focal point of the nearby historic reserve on Turuturu Road. A good coffee is to be had at The Café on Princes Street, next to the Post Office.

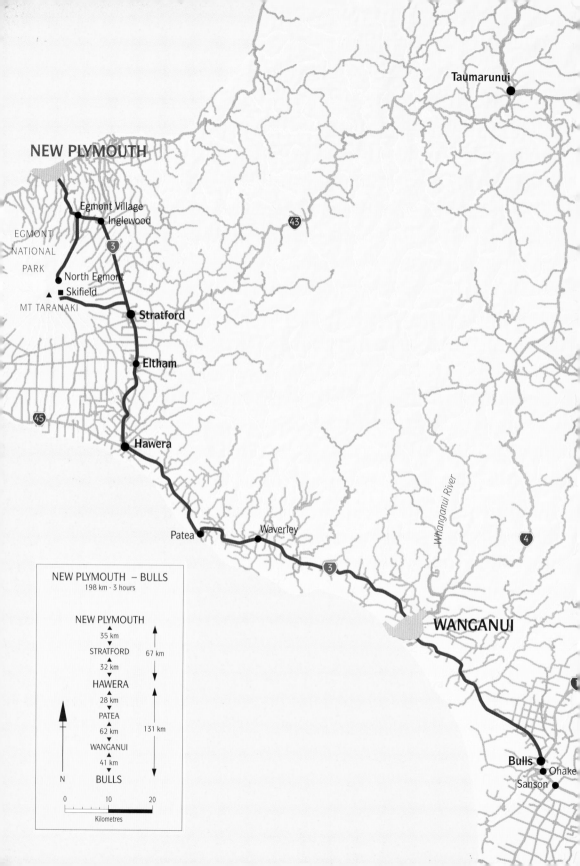

Taumarunui

NEW PLYMOUTH

Egmont Village
Inglewood

EGMONT
NATIONAL
PARK

North Egmont
Skifield

MT TARANAKI

43

3

Stratford

Eltham

45

Hawera

Patea

Waverley

3

Whanganui River

4

WANGANUI

Bulls
Ohake
Sanson

NEW PLYMOUTH – BULLS
198 km - 3 hours

NEW PLYMOUTH
▲
35 km
▼
STRATFORD   67 km
▲
32 km
▼
HAWERA
▲
28 km
▼
PATEA
▲
62 km   131 km
▼
WANGANUI
▲
41 km
▼
BULLS

N

0   10   20

Kilometres

New Plymouth–Bulls SH 3
198 km, 3 hours

This is the main touring route south from New Plymouth, across the ringplain formed by Mt Taranaki, and then along coastal plains, dunelands and hill country to Bulls. With numerous towns, small settlements and the city of Wanganui *en route*, there is no lack of facilities for travellers.

On the outskirts of New Plymouth is the Meeting of the Waters Scenic Reserve, a good place for a picnic, walks in native forest and swimming. Further down the road at Egmont Village (12 km from New Plymouth) is the excellent Kauri Cottage café and the turnoff to North Egmont Visitor Centre in Egmont National Park.

North Egmont, Mt Taranaki – walks
Twenty minutes from Egmont Village, after a narrow winding drive through the forests of Egmont National Park, the road emerges at the bushline at North Egmont. There is an excellent park visitor centre and café here, several forest and alpine walks and fine views of the surrounds and the North Taranaki coast.

Stratford – walks
Back on SH 3, kids would no doubt enjoy the toy factory at Inglewood, otherwise it's a straight run through to Stratford. Signposted at the northern end of the town is the Pembroke Road access to East Egmont. The sealed road (access to Manganui Skifield) climbs well beyond the forest edge to the Stratford Plateau (1100 m) for commanding views of the region, coastline and, on a clear day, the central North Island volcanoes. Back down the mountain there's a shop at the mountain house and forest walks.

Just south of Stratford is the Taranaki Pioneer Village project, a replica village offering visitors a slice of pioneering history.

Eltham – walks
Eltham, like Hawera (see Route 28), has many historic buildings, some of which are over 100 years old. You can see these for yourself by picking up the Historic Eltham brochure from any of the Taranaki visitor centres and following the self-guided heritage walk. Speciality cheeses produced by the local industry can be tasted and bought from the Cheese Bar on Bridge Street.

Hawera (see also Route 28)
Three kilometres south of Hawera is the largest dairy factory in the Southern Hemisphere, run by the Kiwi Cooperative Dairy Company. Although you can't tour the factory, the adjacent Dairylands Visitor Centre and museum is surprisingly good value. Taranaki is first and foremost dairying country and Dairylands is the place to learn more about this industry, with its interactive displays, and even a simulated milk tanker ride in a full size model tanker! Kids love it. There's a café here too.

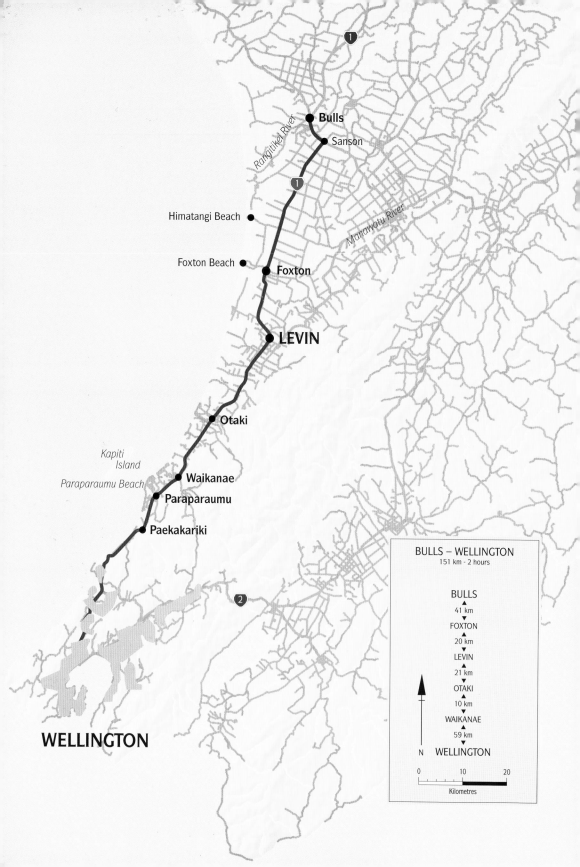

Bulls

Sanson

1

Rangitikei River

Himatangi Beach

Manawatu River

Foxton Beach

Foxton

LEVIN

Otaki

Kapiti Island

Waikanae

Paraparaumu Beach

Paraparaumu

Paekakariki

2

WELLINGTON

BULLS – WELLINGTON
151 km - 2 hours

BULLS
▲
41 km
▼
FOXTON
▲
20 km
▼
LEVIN
▲
21 km
▼
OTAKI
▲
10 km
▼
WAIKANAE
▲
59 km
▼
N   WELLINGTON

0   10   20
Kilometres

Hawera–Wanganui

Allow an hour between Wanganui and Hawera, a trip which passes through Patea and Waverley and many small country settlements. The drive along coastal plains and hill country is pleasant enough, and Patea Beach is worth visiting for walks, a picnic or to let the kids loose in the playground. Waverley's Big Sun café has been recommended.

Wanganui

Wanganui is a river city with a rich Maori and European history, particularly in times when the Whanganui River was the main route to the central North Island. The city's regional museum, Virginia Lake on Wanganui's northwestern outskirts, the Sarjeant Art Gallery and Moutoa Gardens on the banks of the Whanganui River provide reasons to take a break here. The attractively restored historic precinct at the river end of Victoria Avenue has a number of cafés to choose from, while on Moana Ave is the recommended Left Bank Café. SH 4 (the Parapara road) leads north from Wanganui to Tongariro National Park.

Bulls

Bulls, at the junction of SH 1 and SH 3 (about 40 minutes from Wanganui), is well-known for its antique shops and the Ohakea Air Force Museum towards Sanson.

Bulls–Wellington SH 1
151 km, 2 hours

Traffic is noticeably heavier beyond Bulls, particularly at weekends. South of Sanson on the coastal plains between the Rangitikei and Manawatu rivers is the lengthy Foxton straight, notorious for speeding drivers. Highlights include side journeys to beaches at Himatangi, Foxton, Otaki, Waikanae, Paraparaumu and Paekakariki, and several worthwhile museums and galleries.

At Otaki the beautiful Rangiatea Church on Te Rauparaha Road is a highly recommended and nationally significant example of Maori craftsmanship and colonial architecture, which has recently been restored after a fire destroyed the original building. Otaki's new Bank Heritage Museum and Waikanae's Mahara Gallery regularly hold regional and touring exhibitions, while the entertaining Hyde Park Museum at Te Horo is one of several examples in the area of informal collections of nineteenth- and twentieth-century curios and collectables. Lastly, the Southward Car Museum at Otaihanga is outstanding.

There are several good cafés on this stretch: recommended are the Laughing Fox at Foxton, Brown Sugar (at the south end of Otaki), Café Stromboli at Te Horo and Cava at Paraparaumu Beach.

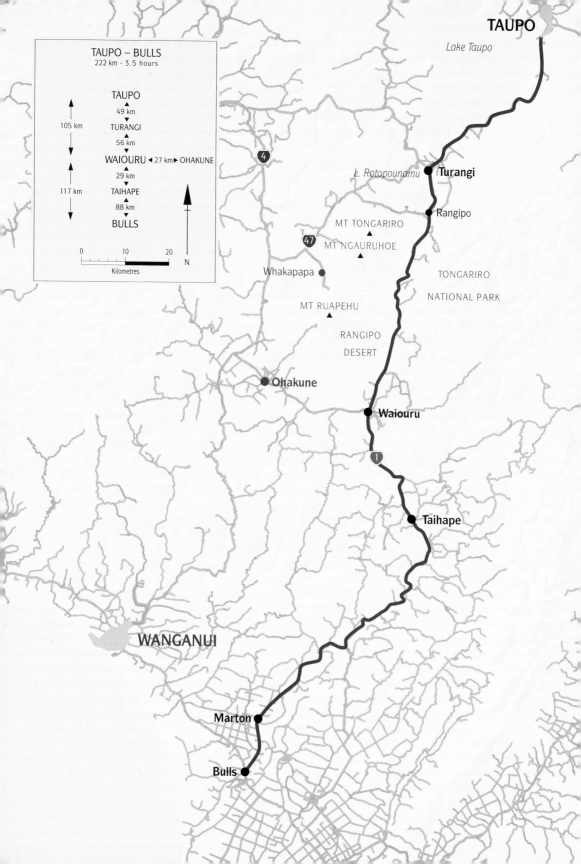

TAUPO

Lake Taupo

TAUPO – BULLS
222 km - 3.5 hours

TAUPO
49 km
TURANGI
56 km
WAIOURU ◄ 27 km ► OHAKUNE
29 km
TAIHAPE
88 km
BULLS

105 km

117 km

0   10   20
Kilometres

N

L. Rotopounamu ● **Turangi**

● Rangipo

MT TONGARIRO ▲

MT NGAURUHOE ▲

TONGARIRO

NATIONAL PARK

Whakapapa ●

MT RUAPEHU ▲

RANGIPO
DESERT

● **Ohakune**

● **Waiouru**

①

● **Taihape**

WANGANUI

Marton ●

Bulls ●

Taupo–Bulls SH 1
222 km, 3.5 hours

The scenic highlights of this route are provided by the 105-km drive around Lake Taupo and along the Desert Road past the Tongariro volcanoes to Waiouru. Beyond here interest pales unless you've a penchant for rural scenery. SH 1 is the North Island's busiest highway and fuel and refreshments are available at most centres.

Turangi – campground, walks
The drive to Turangi stays close to the lakeshore and there are many beaches, picnic sites and walks (see DoC's *Taupo Walks* brochure) to enjoy. Turangi has a very good information centre, and fish and chip fans should try a legendary hamburger from Grand Central Fry on Ohuanga Road. Across the road is the excellent Mustard Seed Café.

SH 47 between Turangi and National Park offers fine views of the Tongariro volcanoes and a number of good short walk opportunities which are covered by a DoC brochure. The Lake Rotopounamu forest walk 11 km from Turangi is recommended for its picnic sites and swimming. The turnoff to Whakapapa (see Hamilton–Wanganui, Route 17) is 40 km from Turangi.

The Desert Road
SH 1 between Turangi and Waiouru involves crossing the Rangipo Desert. The route's outstanding mountain scenery is best experienced in the morning when the volcanoes are lit by the sun. In winter (and sometimes summer) the road can be closed by snowfall.

Lake Taupo

Waiouru
The Waiouru Army Museum employs audio-visual presentations and static displays of military hardware and photography to recount New Zealand's military history from nineteenth-century land wars to contemporary UN peacekeeping. Far from glorifying the military, the account is often moving. Waiouru's best café is in the foyer. If travelling east, allow 30 minutes to reach Ohakune by SH 49.

Waiouru–Bulls
This section requires about two hours. Taihape is the largest centre between Taupo and Bulls, servicing both the local, rural and tourist markets. Eating options have improved markedly in recent years on this leg of SH 1: try Taihape's Café Exchange and Brown Sugar Café, Annabelle's Café in Hunterville, and Coffee Rush in Bulls (drive through the village to the Rangitikei River bridge).

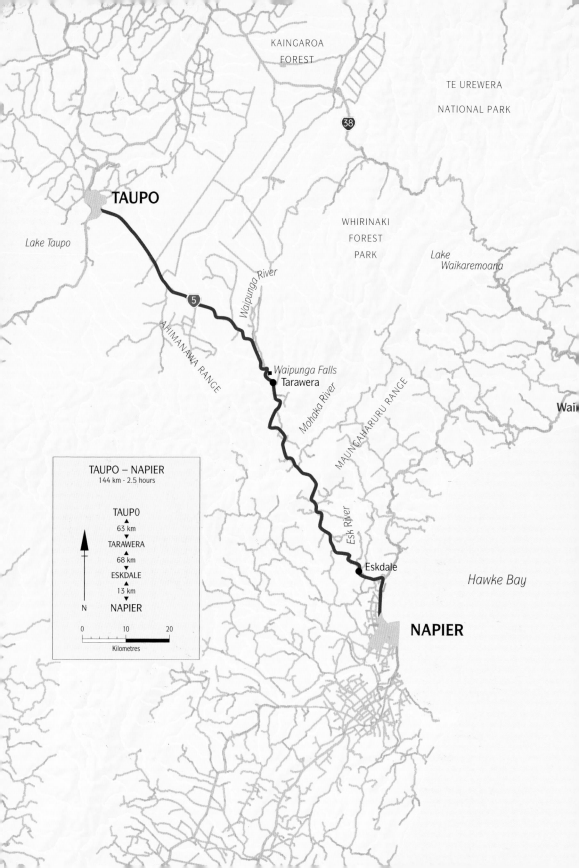

KAINGAROA
FOREST

TE UREWERA

NATIONAL PARK

38

TAUPO

Lake Taupo

WHIRINAKI

FOREST

PARK

*Lake
Waikaremoana*

Waipunga River

5

AHIMANAWA RANGE

■ *Waipunga Falls*
Tarawera

Mohaka River

MAUNGAHARURU RANGE

Wai

Esk River

● Eskdale

Hawke Bay

NAPIER

TAUPO – NAPIER
144 km - 2.5 hours

TAUPO
▲
63 km
▼
TARAWERA
▲
68 km
▼
ESKDALE
▲
13 km
▼
NAPIER

N

0   10   20

Kilometres

Taupo–Napier SH 5, 2
144 km, 2 hours

Once a bush trail used by central North Island Maori and a two-day stagecoach ride in colonial times, these days the Napier–Taupo highway is entirely sealed and far from the wild ride it was even in the 1960s and 70s. The road crosses rough and remote terrain as it cuts through the Ahimanawa Range and descends from the Volcanic Plateau towards Hawke Bay.

17 km from Taupo is the start of the Northern Loop track (30-45 minutes) in the Opepe Scenic and Historic Reserve (see DoC's *Taupo Walks* brochure), notable for its remnant of mature forest which has survived volcanic eruptions, fires and logging. Waipunga Falls lookout is 49 km from Taupo in the Waipunga Valley shortly before Tarawera settlement.

The route then crosses the Mohaka River, climbs the Maungaharuru Range (very good views of the surrounding country) and descends to the Esk Valley wine growing area, meeting SH 2 at Bay View, 10 minutes north of Napier.

There are tearooms at Tarawera and Te Haroto, and more sophisticated offerings at wineries in the Esk Valley, and towards Napier.

Waipunga Falls

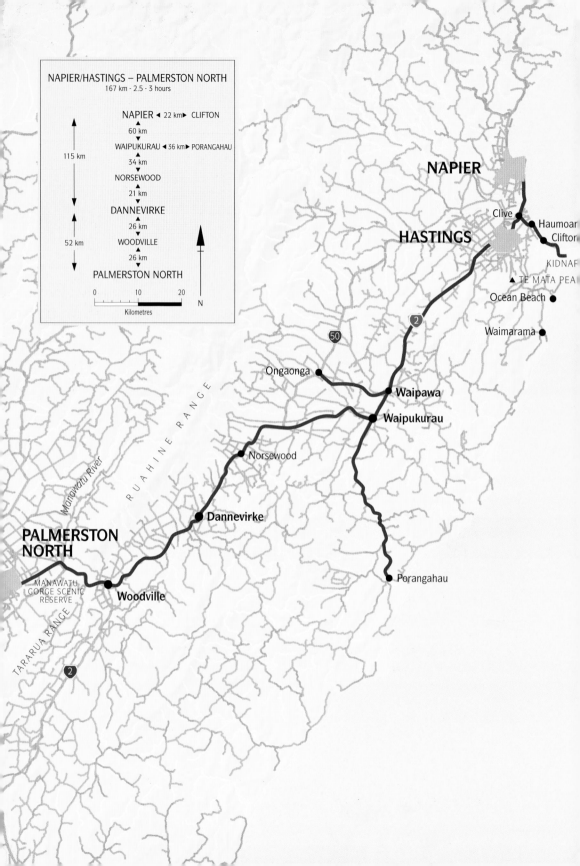

NAPIER/HASTINGS – PALMERSTON NORTH
167 km - 2.5 - 3 hours

NAPIER ◀ 22 km ▶ CLIFTON
▲
60 km
▼
WAIPUKURAU ◀ 36 km ▶ PORANGAHAU
34 km
NORSEWOOD
21 km
DANNEVIRKE
26 km
WOODVILLE
26 km
PALMERSTON NORTH

115 km

52 km

0   10   20

Kilometres

N

NAPIER

HASTINGS

Clive

Haumoar
Clifton

KIDNAF

TE MATA PEA

Ocean Beach

Waimarama

Ongaonga

Waipawa

Waipukurau

2

50

Norsewood

Dannevirke

PALMERSTON
NORTH

MANAWATU
GORGE SCENIC
RESERVE

Woodville

Porangahau

RUAHINE RANGE

Manawatu River

TARARUA RANGE

2

Napier/Hastings–Palmerston North SH 2, 3
167 km, 2.5–3 hours

South of Napier and Hastings, SH 2 rolls through the dry country landscapes east of the Ruahine Range. Sheep farming is the major industry, but farm forestry, winemaking and market gardening are prominent too. Locals recommend scenic drives to Te Mata Peak, Ocean Beach and Waimarama southwest of Hastings, and to Porangahau, south of Waipukarau. The most popular diversion, however, is the trip to Cape Kidnappers.

Cape Kidnappers Gannet Reserve – campground, walks, picnicking
The Cape Kidnappers Gannet Reserve contains New Zealand's largest colony of Australasian gannets. November to late February is the best time to visit – public access is closed between July and October. To reach the colony turn off SH 2 just beyond Clive (10 km from Napier) and make for the coast at Haumoana and drive on toward Clifton (12 km). Art and craft galleries, wineries and cafés are well established between Haumoana and Clifton (Clifton's Clifton Bay Café is the pick of the eating establishments). The beach walk to the Cape (5 hours return) and most guided tours by vehicle begin at Scotsmans Point just short of Clifton (campground). You need to check the tides before setting out on the walk. An informative DoC brochure is available from visitor centres.

Waipawa/Waipukurau/Ongaonga
Twenty minutes from Hastings on SH 2 is the excellent Paper Mulberry Café (organic wholefoods and good coffee), while on the outskirts of Waipawa is the Abbotslee Historic Homestead and tearooms where you can enjoy fine home cooking in a gracious setting. At the south end of Waipukurau is another fine travellers café – Hatuma Café.

Waipawa and Waipukurau are bustling service towns. Waipawa's Settlers Museum is its main attraction, but for a real sense of the region's settler history the diversion west to Ongaonga (on SH 50, 17 km from Waipawa) features numerous preserved historic buildings, 11 of which are listed with the New Zealand Historic Places Trust. (SH 50 between Takapau and Napier is covered by a Heritage Trail brochure.)

Norsewood/Dannevirke
In the hills at the base of the Ruahine Range, the tiny village of Norsewood reflects its Scandinavian heritage in its Pioneer Museum, a kids' troll trail and the country's smallest cheese factory – Rangiuru Farm – where you can sample and buy from a range of delicious organic cheeses. The Norsewear factory on Hovding Street has a shop where you can buy from their famous range of woollen knitwear. In Dannevirke the hungry and thirsty can visit the State of the Art Café on the main street.

Manawatu Gorge – walks
West of Woodville, SH 3 jags toward Palmerston North through the Manawatu Gorge Scenic Reserve between the Ruahine and Tararua ranges. Two short forest walks begin at the Woodville end of the reserve.

From Palmerston North, SH 3 runs north to connect with SH 1 south of Bulls, while travelling south SH 57 connects with SH 1 near Levin. (See Bulls–Wellington, Route 30)

PALMERSTON NORTH

Woodville

Mangatainoka

Pahiatua

Eketahuna

Mount Bruce

LEVIN

Kapiti Island

Manawatu River

RUAHINE RANGES

Ruamahanga R.

T A R A R U A   R A N G E

Waiohine River

MASTERTON

Castlepoint

Carterton

Greytown

Featherston

Martinborough

WELLINGTON

Lake Wairarapa

R I M U T A K A   R A N G E

Lake Ferry

Whangaimoana

Putangirua Pinnacles

HAURANGI

FOREST PARK

A O R A N G I   R A N G E

Palliser Bay

TE HUMENGA PT

Ngawi

CAPE PALLISER

WOODVILLE – WELLINGTON
177 km · 3-4 hours

WOODVILLE
▲
40 km
EKETAHUNA
▲
42 km
MASTERTON ◄ 60 km ►
CASTLEPOINT
▲
37 km
FEATHERSTON ◄ 18 km ►
MARTINBOROUGH
▲
58 km
WELLINGTON

82 km ↕

95 km ↕

N

0   10   20
Kilometres

Woodville–Wellington SH 2
177 km, 3–4 hours

Of the two routes to Wellington from Woodville (the other being via Palmerston North, Shannon and Levin on SH 56 or 57, 2.5 hours), this route east of the Tararua Range through Wairarapa's wide river valleys and undulating hill country offers more varied and interesting travelling.

Wairarapa's highlights include the Department of Conservation's National Wildlife Centre at Mount Bruce and rewarding drives to the coast at Castlepoint and Palliser Bay. In southern Wairarapa craft artists, clothes designers, winemakers and restaurateurs have made the most of Wairarapa's proximity to Wellington and established a boutique shopping and café culture that has enlivened Masterton, Featherston, Greytown and Martinborough. The preservation of colonial buildings, especially in Greytown, has done much to enhance the character of these southern towns. You will find a succinct account of the region's Maori and European history in the very good *Heritage Trails of Wairarapa* booklet (free at visitor centres).

Mangatainoka/Pahiatua

Nine kilometres from Woodville, beer boffins will enjoy a tour of Mangatainoka's main attraction, the Tui Brewery. Bookings are required. Further up the Mangatainoka River is Pahiatua, a town that began as a nineteenth-century roading camp in the vast totara forest that once extended between Mount Bruce and Takapau in central Hawke's Bay. 'Forty Mile Bush', as the tract between Mount Bruce and Woodville was named, was felled from the 1870s by Scandinavian immigrants contracted by the colonial government for their tree-felling and roadbuilding skills. One can only marvel at their thoroughness as you drive south through what has become prosperous sheep and dairy farming country.

Mt Bruce National Wildlife Centre – walks

The largest remnant of Forty Mile Bush occurs 17 km south of Eketahuna at Mount Bruce. Since 1962 this 945 ha reserve has been the home of the Mt Bruce National Wildlife Centre, a captive-rearing facility central to efforts to prevent the extinction of many of New Zealand's endangered birds, including takahe, kokako, stitchbird and the Campbell Island teal. Birds reared here are eventually released on offshore reserves such as Kapiti Island, or back to the wild to bolster struggling populations.

Takahe, Mt Bruce

For the public, the centre is an excellent educational facility which utilises displays, videos, and an audio-visual presentation to outline its work and the Department of Conservation's endangered species recovery programmes. Many of the endangered birds can be viewed in specially constructed forest aviaries, while brown kiwi and tuatara are housed in indoor facilities.

Easy walks through the forest of tall totara, rimu, kahikatea and tawa are likely to bring sightings of other more common forest birds. A special treat will be a sighting of North Island kaka (a large forest parrot) which have been successfully released into the forest. Kaka are fed daily at 3 p.m. as part of a supplementary feeding programme. And if you're in need of a supplementary feed yourself, there's a café at the centre.

Masterton

From Mount Bruce SH 2 crosses a spur that falls from the Tararua Range, then descends the Ruamahanga Valley to Masterton, Wairarapa's main commercial centre. Turn off at the northern end of the town for the drive to Castlepoint (see below). Café options in Masterton include Café Strada (main street) and the excellent Slow Food Café on the southern outskirts. Café Trocadero is attached to Aratoi, Wairarapa's regional museum and gallery on Bruce Street.

Carterton/Greytown/Featherston – picnicking

Rural decline and loss of key industries have greatly affected these small rural service centres, but Greytown and Featherston have done well by refocusing on the visitor industry and heritage tourism. Carterton's Wild Oats café and bakery is recommended, otherwise push through to Greytown.

The Waiohine Gorge, ten minutes north of Greytown is a popular recreational and picnicking area. Greytown residents and entrepreneurs have retained the town's colonial character by enhancing its classic wooden Victorian buildings, many of which now house cafés, galleries and antique shops. Papawai marae occupied an important place in New Zealand's history when it was home to the Kotahitanga (Maori Parliament) movement in the 1890s.

Featherston, at the base of the Rimutaka Range, has like Greytown retained many of its Victorian buildings, a number of which have New Zealand Historic Places Trust listings. Along with galleries and cafés (the Lady Featherston café is the pick of them), Featherston's Heritage Museum is well worth a visit.

Rimutaka Range to Wellington
1 hour

Allow an hour to reach Wellington from Featherston over the Rimutaka Range. While the highway is narrow in places there are numerous passing lanes. Snow or particularly bad weather can lead to road closures. There are toilets at the top of the range at the Summit Café and a passable café at Kaitoke Country Gardens, but it's probably worth carrying on to Petone on the edge of Wellington Harbour where several standout cafés are located on Jackson Street – including the Palace and Caffiend.

Featherston–Martinborough and Cape Palliser
1 hour

Martinborough

Martinborough is 15 minutes from Featherston via SH 53. Alternatively, you can bypass Featherston by taking a route direct from Greytown. Martinborough's ascent as a premiere winemaking region has boosted the town's popularity, particularly with weekend visitors from the capital. The Martinborough fairs in February and March draw tens of thousands of people. At other times of the year you can sample the region's wines, in particular its outstanding Pinot Noir, at the Martinborough Wine Centre or at boutique vineyards within walking distance from the town. Medici Café is recommended for lunches, or if you just want a coffee to go, go to the Post Office!

Palliser Bay – campground, walks, swimming, picnicking

The route to the coast at Palliser Bay begins at the Martinborough Square and skirts the Aorangi Range in Haurangi Forest Park. Shortly before Lake Ferry (motorcamp) the route turns toward Whangaimoana. The road winds for a short time above the bay offering views across Cook Strait to the South Island. When the road reaches the coast at Te Kopi look for the start of the track to the Putangirua Pinnacles (2 hours return, camping), an impressive area formed by 'badlands' erosion which featured in *Return of the King* – the third film in the Lord of the Rings trilogy.

Eastern Palliser Bay has a long history of human occupation. There are burial sites all along this coast, while rock walls dating to the 12th century at Te Humenga Point are among the earliest evidence of Maori settlement in New Zealand. After Te Kopi the road follows the coast to Cape Palliser, much of the way being unsealed. There's a shop at the extraordinary Ngawi fishing village where the fleet is hauled ashore by tractor. Cape Palliser lighthouse is a short distance from Ngawi and the great slabs of rock called Kupe's Sails – said to be the sails that powered the canoe of Kupe, the Polynesian voyager. Seals from a nearby colony, the largest in the North Island, loll about on the rocks and in tidal pools. There are plenty of places to picnic and enjoy the coastal scenery.

Masterton–Castlepoint – campground, swimming, picnicking
1 hour

Castlepoint, another favourite Wairarapa coastal haunt, is reached via a pleasant drive through the region's eastern hill country. The route (sealed) begins at a signposted junction on the northern edge of Masterton. Tinui has a hotel and store. At Castlepoint village are spectacular cliff and headland walks, beach and safe lagoon-swimming options and picnicking.

Castlepoint

South Island Routes   Page

35	Picton – Nelson SH 6 & Queen Charlotte Drive	78
36	Nelson – Farewell Spit SH 6, 60	80
37	Motueka – Kohatu Junction SH 61	83
38	Nelson – Westport SH 6	84
39	Westport – Karamea SH 67	86
40	Westport – Greymouth SH 6	88
41	Westport – Greymouth via Reefton SH 6, 69, 7	89
42	Murchison – Christchurch via Lewis Pass SH 65, 7, 1	90
43	Greymouth – Fox Glacier SH 6	94
44	Fox Glacier – Wanaka via Haast Pass SH 6	98
45	Picton – Christchurch SH 1	102
46	Banks Peninsula: Christchurch – Akaroa via Port Hills & SH 75	106
47	Woodend – Geraldine SH 72	108
48	Christchurch – Greymouth via Arthur's Pass SH 73, 6	110
49	Christchurch – Dunedin SH 1	114
50	Omarama – Oamaru SH 83	118
51	Christchurch – Wanaka SH 1, 79, 8	120
52	Wanaka – Queenstown SH 6 & Crown Range Road	124
53	Queenstown – Milford Sound SH 6, 94	126
54	Queenstown – Dunedin via Clutha Valley SH 8	130
55	Cromwell – Dunedin via Middlemarch SH 8, 85, 87	132
56	Dunedin – Invercargill SH 1	134
57	Balclutha – Invercargill via the Catlins Coast SH 92	136
58	Te Anau – Invercargill via Tuatapere SH 95, 99	140

Collingwood

36

37

35 Picton

Karamea

Nelson

39

38 Blenheim

Westport

38 Murchison

40

42

Punakaiki

45

41

Greymouth

42

Arthur's
Pass

Kaikoura

45

48

43

47 Woodend

Fox Glacier

47 Christchurch

Mount Cook

49

46

44

51

Geraldine

Tekapo

Timaru

Omarama

Milford Sound

51

49

Wanaka

50

Queenstown 52

Oamaru

53

55

Cromwell

Te Anau

53

54

49

58

Dunedin

56

Invercargill

56

Balclutha

57

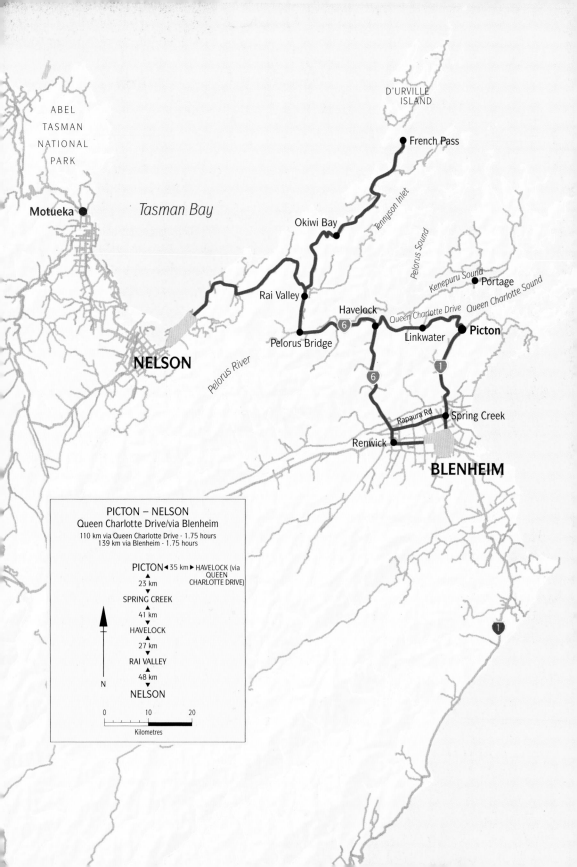

ABEL
TASMAN
NATIONAL
PARK

Motueka

Tasman Bay

D'URVILLE
ISLAND

French Pass

Okiwi Bay

Tennyson Inlet

Pelorus Sound

Kenepuru Sound

Portage

Rai Valley

Havelock

Queen Charlotte Drive   Queen Charlotte Sound

Pelorus Bridge

Linkwater

Picton

NELSON

Pelorus River

Rapaura Rd

Spring Creek

Renwick

BLENHEIM

PICTON – NELSON
Queen Charlotte Drive/via Blenheim
110 km via Queen Charlotte Drive - 1.75 hours
139 km via Blenheim - 1.75 hours

PICTON ◄35 km► HAVELOCK (via
QUEEN
CHARLOTTE DRIVE)

23 km

SPRING CREEK

41 km

HAVELOCK

27 km

RAI VALLEY

48 km

NELSON

N

0   10   20
Kilometres

Picton–Nelson SH 6/Queen Charlotte Drive
110 km via Queen Charlotte Drive, 1.75 hours
139 km via Blenheim (Rapaura Rd), 1.75 hours

Queen Charlotte Drive is the most scenic route to Nelson, however driving along the Rapaura Road route takes you into the heart of the Marlborough wine growing area. *The Treasured Pathway* (Nikau Press) offers informed coverage of the natural and cultural features experienced along either of these routes.

Queen Charlotte Drive – campgrounds, walks, swimming, boating
Queen Charlotte Drive begins in Picton (signposted off SH 1). This picturesque 35 km drive links Queen Charlotte and Pelorus sounds before joining SH 6 at Havelock. Narrow and winding at times, the road has several lookouts over the sounds and passes sublime forest-fringed bays with safe beaches and seaside campgrounds in Grove Arm. For a leg-stretcher or picnic site, visit Anakiwa (turn right at Linkwater) at the southern end of the Queen Charlotte Walkway.

Nelson via Rapaura Rd – wineries, fruit stalls
Turning west along Rapaura Road (leave SH 1 about 23 km south of Picton at Spring Creek) is quicker than driving into Blenheim and immediately places you in Marlborough's world famous wine-growing area. In the space of 15 km come numerous wineries – among them Hunters, Selaks, Nautilus, Cloudy Bay, Allan Scott and Babich – offering tastings, wine sales and cafés. Rapaura Road meets SH 6 to Nelson just before Renwick (tearooms, supermarket, petrol etc). Driving back towards Blenheim offers more wineries and fruit stalls.

Havelock – campground, boating
The fishing village of Havelock, at the head of Pelorus Sound, is now a thriving tourist village with several cafés and curio stores. Try Mussel Boys restaurant if you want to sample the local marine produce.

Pelorus Bridge Scenic Reserve – campground, walks, picnicking, swimming
20 km from Havelock, this remnant lowland forest on the banks of the Pelorus River has been a travellers' waypoint for over 100 years. There's a great swimming hole, several short forest walks, and the café serves home-cooked food and good coffee.

From Pelorus Bridge, SH 6 passes through Rai Valley (tearooms, dairy, petrol), then crosses the Rai and Whangamoa saddles, a landscape dominated by the region's plantation forests. At the bottom of the Whangamoa, just past Hira, the road crests a hill to reveal wonderful views across Tasman Bay to the Abel Tasman coastline and the mountains of Kahurangi National Park.

Tennyson Inlet/French Pass
Just beyond Rai Valley a road leads off to the beautiful Tennyson Inlet (1 hour, last few kilometres unsealed from Opouri Saddle) and to French Pass (2 hours, unsealed from Okiwi Bay) in outer Pelorus Sound.

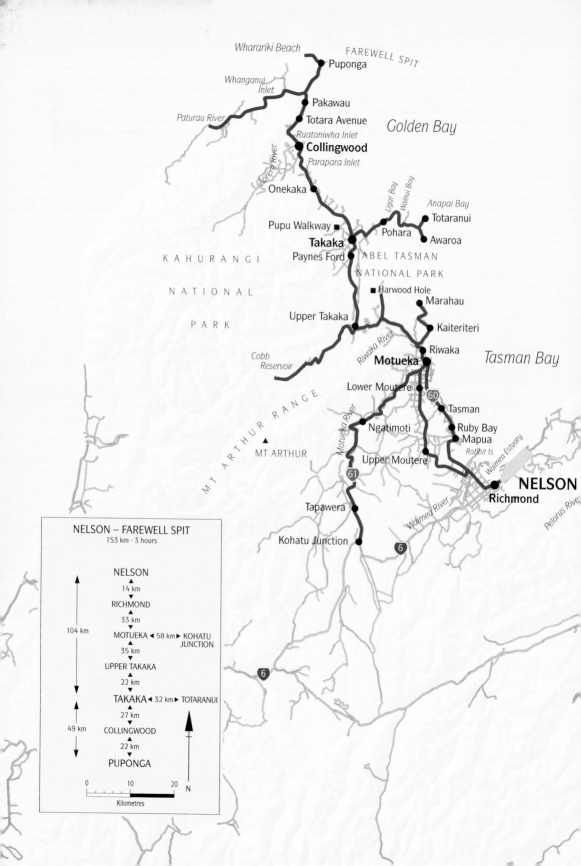

Wharariki Beach

FAREWELL SPIT

Puponga

Whanganui Inlet

Pakawau

Totara Avenue

Ruataniwha Inlet

Paturau River

Collingwood

Parapara Inlet

Golden Bay

Onekaka

Aorere River

Ligar Bay

Wainui Bay

Anapai Bay

Pupu Walkway

Pohara

Totaranui

Takaka

Awaroa

Paynes Ford

ABEL TASMAN

KAHURANGI

NATIONAL PARK

Harwood Hole

Marahau

NATIONAL

Upper Takaka

Kaiteriteri

PARK

Riwaka

Tasman Bay

Cobb Reservoir

Riwaka River

Motueka

Lower Moutere

60

M T A R T H U R   R A N G E

Motueka River

Ngatimoti

Tasman

Ruby Bay

Mapua

▲ MT ARTHUR

Upper Moutere

Rabbit Is.

Waimea Estuary

61

NELSON

Tapawera

Waimea River

Richmond

Pelorus River

Kohatu Junction

6

6

NELSON – FAREWELL SPIT
153 km · 3 hours

NELSON
▲
14 km
▼
RICHMOND
▲
33 km
▼
MOTUEKA ◄ 58 km ► KOHATU
JUNCTION
▲
35 km
▼
UPPER TAKAKA
▲
22 km
▼
TAKAKA ◄ 32 km ► TOTARANUI
▲
27 km
▼
COLLINGWOOD
▲
22 km
▼
PUPONGA

104 km

49 km

0   10   20
Kilometres

N

Nelson–Farewell Spit SH 6, 60
153 km, 3 hours

This drive combines all that makes a visit to Nelson and Golden Bay so memorable – beaches, mountain scenery and forest walks, craft galleries, wineries and cafés. Two regional guides *Art in Its Own Place* and *The Treasured Pathway* will greatly enhance the journey across the Waimea Plains, over Takaka Hill's marble landscape, and into the quieter recesses of Golden Bay. Pamphlets are available on the walks noted below from information centres.

Nelson, Richmond and environs

Nelson city brims with cafés and restaurants (highly recommended are Broccoli Row, The Cut or Morrison Street Café in the central city, or The Boatshed on the waterfront). Continuing south on SH 6 you soon reach Stoke, location of the World of WearableArt (WoW) Gallery – the must-visit centre of Nelson's internationally renowned Montana WoW Awards Show. There is a good café here, and the classic car museum next door is also a popular attraction.

Richmond is 14 km south of Nelson on SH 6 on the edge of Waimea Estuary and the Waimea Plains. SH 60 turns toward Motueka and Golden Bay at a roundabout south of Richmond. Between Richmond and Mapua are numerous wineries, cafés and craft galleries (all well signposted), notably Waimea Estate's Café in the Vineyard, Seifried Estate winery and Silkwood Arts and Crafts. Redwood Road, 6 km from Richmond, leads to Rabbit Island, one of the region's best beaches.

Mapua/Ruby Bay/Tasman

SH 60 allows glimpses of Waimea Estuary as you travel toward Mapua – a pleasant seaside hamlet at the mouth of Waimea Estuary which has several cafés, including the long established Smokehouse Café and the newer Flax – both are outstanding. Try also the Naked Bun bakery and café for their sophisticated take on pastries (I am reliably informed their custard squares are 'phenomenal'), cakes and breads. Mapua's aquarium is also highly recommended.

Ruby Bay has the funky Flying Fish café for takeaway or eat-in curry and pizza, and a couple of excellent winery cafés nearby, including Ruby Bay Wines. Tasman's Jester House café, with its spacious garden, playground and tame eels, has long been a family favourite, and the food is great too.

Motueka – campground

After Tasman and the drive around Moutere Inlet you reach Motueka (45 minutes from Nelson) where you can take a break at the Arcadia Organic Café or Hot Mama's Café (on the right side of the main street). Motueka's swimming beach and salt water baths are on Wharf Road (turn right at the roundabout on the southern edge of the town).

Richmond–Motueka via the 'Moutere Highway'

This alternative inland route, with views of the Mt Arthur Range, is sometimes quicker than the busier SH 60. It turns off SH 60 just past the Waimea River bridge. Kahurangi Winery Café is located just before Upper Moutere, while

Neudorf Vineyard is located north of Upper Moutere village. The excellent Riverside Café is on the outskirts of Motueka at Lower Moutere.

Kaiteriteri/Marahau (Abel Tasman National Park) – campground, walks, picnicking, swimming, kayaking

After Motueka, SH 60 crosses the Motueka River and leads toward Abel Tasman National Park and Takaka Hill. Real fruit ice creams and organic fruit can be bought from roadside stalls. Shortly after Riwaka village, roads lead from SH 60 to Kaiteriteri Beach and Marahau. Marahau, 20 minutes over a hill from SH 60, is at the southern entrance to Abel Tasman National Park and is the base for sea kayaking, launch tours and day walks in the park. The park's renowned beaches and coastal forests can be sampled on Tinline Walk and the return trip to Coquille Bay (both 1 hour), but don't expect solitude. There are now two cafés here, including the new Hooked on Marahau.

Takaka Hill – walks, views

The summit of Takaka Hill is a fascinating landscape of water-etched marble outcrops, sinkholes and caves. Though it is a slow grind to the top (prone to slips in bad weather, and ice and occasional snow in winter) there are several rewarding walks and viewpoints over Tasman and Golden Bays. These include the source of the Riwaka River (at the base of the hill); Hawke's Lookout, a short walk from SH 60 close to the summit; and the walk to Harwood Hole – a spectacular 176 m shaft – which begins 15 km down Canaan Road (signposted) in Abel Tasman National Park. Take care on the narrow gravel road, and allow 1.5 hours for the walk. Before the road descends to the Takaka Valley is the new Takaka Hill Walkway (2–3 hours) and Harwood Lookout with outstanding views of Kahurangi National Park.

Upper Takaka/Cobb Valley – campground, walks, picnicking

A turn left at Upper Takaka leads up the Takaka River to the Cobb Power Station, and thereafter up a steep unsealed road to the Cobb Reservoir where there are several interesting day walk possibilities onto the Peel Range or to Lake Sylvester. Allow 1 hour to the reservoir. The road is often narrow and winding, and not recommended for campervans.

Takaka – campground

Just before Takaka is Paynes Ford Scenic Reserve, a top rock climbing area, though it's the swimming hole here that attracts most people. Takaka (1 hour from Motueka) in high summer is the vibrant centre of Golden Bay, with its craft outlets, weekend market and eateries. The Wholemeal Café is an excellent Takaka institution but several good new places can also be recommended – the Dangerous Kitchen, Brigands and Eatery on the Rocks (on the Nelson side of Takaka in pleasant garden surrounds).

Takaka–Totaranui (Abel Tasman National Park) – campground, walks, swimming, fishing

Totaranui is 32 km (1 hour) from Takaka. The road passes Pohara Beach (campground, beach) where one of Golden Bay's newest and best cafés is found – the Coffee House and Roastery. From Wainui Bay the road is unsealed (suitable for campervans) as it climbs over a forested range to Totaranui. Apart from the fine beach here, there is a DoC visitor centre, campground and walks toward Awaroa or Anapai bays.

Te Waikoropupu Springs/Pupu Walkway – walks

Back on SH 60, 4 km west of Takaka is the turnoff (at the Waitapu Bridge) to these renowned and quite beautiful springs – the clearest fresh water in the Southern Hemisphere. An easy forest walk past old gold diggings leads to the springs. The springs are sacred to Maori and swimming in them is considered a desecration of their mauri or lifeforce. The Pupu Walkway (2 hours return through mature podocarp forest) is reached via a gravelled road to the springs.

Collingwood – campground, swimming

Between Takaka and Collingwood (27 km) SH 60 stays inland until Parapara Inlet, with viewpoints overlooking Golden Bay, the Abel Tasman coastline and Farewell Spit. Expect good hospitality and food at the Mussel Inn country café and brewery at Onekaka. Collingwood, at the mouth of the Aorere River, is where you organise tours to the Farewell Spit bird sanctuary or transport to the Heaphy Track, and enjoy good food and coffee at the Courthouse Café. For more treats, visit Rosy Glow Chocolates on the beachfront.

Pakawau – campground

From Collingwood SH 60 skirts Ruataniwha Inlet and returns to the coast at Totara Avenue where signs warn the motorist to watch for penguins crossing the road. The road follows a long sweep of beach to Pakawau where there is a popular campground and the Schoolhouse Café. Just past Pakawau a road leads to Whanganui Inlet and Paturau River mouth on the west coast (32 km) – a five-star scenic drive, unsealed.

Puponga/Farewell Spit/Wharariki Beach – walks, picnicking

Farewell Spit Visitor Centre and Café is located a short distance from Puponga on a rise overlooking the spit's high wind-whipped dunelands. Easy walking tracks lead from the centre across Puponga Farm Park to the spit's outer and inner coastlines. The (half-day) clifftop walk toward Wharariki Beach is one of the best in Golden Bay, though the shorter walk to Fossil Point is also rewarded with outstanding scenery.

A 10-minute drive north of Puponga leads to a carpark and 20-minute walk across grassy dunes to the beautiful Wharariki Beach – for many the highlight of a visit to Golden Bay. You can take long walks down the beach, and watch seals in the surf off the spectacular Archway Islands. The track towards Farewell Spit climbs high onto cliffs and within view of seal haul-out zones and nursery areas.

Motueka–Kohatu Junction SH 61
58 km, 1 hour

A useful route to SH 6 for those travelling between Christchurch and Golden Bay. The road follows the eastern flanks of Kahurangi National Park along the Motueka River, an outstanding trout fishing river. Park access: turn off at Ngatimoti for the Mt Arthur road end, and at Tapawera for the Wangapeka Track. Both access roads are unsealed. Tapawera is the largest locality on SH 61, with a garage and store.

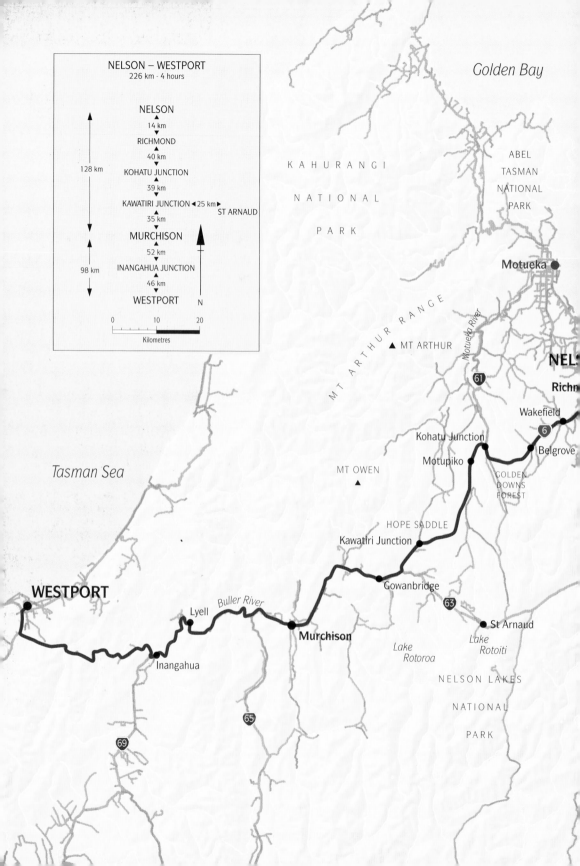

NELSON – WESTPORT
226 km - 4 hours

NELSON
▲
14 km
RICHMOND
▲
40 km
KOHATU JUNCTION
▲
39 km
KAWATIRI JUNCTION ◄25 km►
▲
35 km
MURCHISON
▲
52 km
INANGAHUA JUNCTION
▲
46 km
WESTPORT

128 km

98 km

ST ARNAUD

N

0   10   20
Kilometres

Golden Bay

KAHURANGI

NATIONAL

PARK

ABEL
TASMAN
NATIONAL
PARK

Motueka ●

MT ARTHUR RANGE

▲ MT ARTHUR

Motueka River

NEL*

(61)

Richm

Wakefield

(6)

Kohatu Junction

Belgrove

Motupiko

GOLDEN
DOWNS
FOREST

MT OWEN
▲

HOPE SADDLE

Kawatiri Junction

Tasman Sea

Gowanbridge

(63)

WESTPORT

Lyell

Buller River

Murchison

St Arnaud
●

*Lake
Rotoroa*

*Lake
Rotoiti*

Inangahua

NELSON LAKES

(65)

NATIONAL

PARK

(69)

Nelson–Westport SH 6
226 km, 4 hours

Allow a day to enjoy this drive to the West Coast. Highlights are the crossing of Hope Saddle and the journey through the forested scenic reserves and earthquake-riven landscapes of the Buller Gorge. SH 6 also provides access to Nelson Lakes National Park.

Nelson–Kawatiri Junction – views, picnicking
Quick progress is made south of Nelson city past Richmond and several small rural centres to Belgrove. Past here SH 6 climbs to the crest of the Spooners Range in the heart of the vast Golden Downs pine plantation. (NB: The road that departs Belgrove through Golden Downs Forest to St Arnaud is the fastest route to Nelson Lakes from Nelson city. Allow 1 hour.) SH 6 meets SH 61 from Motueka at Kohatu Junction (see Route 37), and thereafter continues up the Motupiko Valley toward Hope Saddle – where there are superb views of Nelson Lakes and the Kahurangi mountains. The Buller River is reached at Kawatiri Junction (picnicking and short walks). SH 63 turns here for St Arnaud (25 km) and Blenheim (127 km, 1.5 hours).

Murchison
From Kawatiri Junction the route closely follows the Buller River as it descends toward Murchison through beech forest reserves and farmed river flats. At Gowanbridge, 6 km from the junction, is the access road (sealed) to Lake Rotoroa. Near Murchison it is worth pausing for the views back toward the grey marble flanks of Mt Owen. Murchison's Rivers Café, at the Adventure Centre on Fairfax Street, still outshines the competition with great coffee and food. The Murchison Museum is worth a look if you have time.

Inangahua
Beyond Murchison the Buller enters a forested gorge with impressive rapids and huge earthquake slips. SH 6 crosses the Buller at O'Sullivans Bridge 11 km from Murchison. A few minutes further on is the somewhat contrived 'swingbridge' attraction. Save your energy for free beech forest walks at Lyell, the site of a nineteenth-century mining town (camping, picnicking and historic relics). At the Inangahua Hall, residents have established a fine historic display that recounts the tremendous earthquakes that devastated the Inangahua/Murchison area in 1928 and 1967.

Buller River

Lower Buller Gorge–Westport
The slow and graceful passage of the Buller between banks of rata forest is a superb finale to this drive as it traces the lower gorge toward Westport.

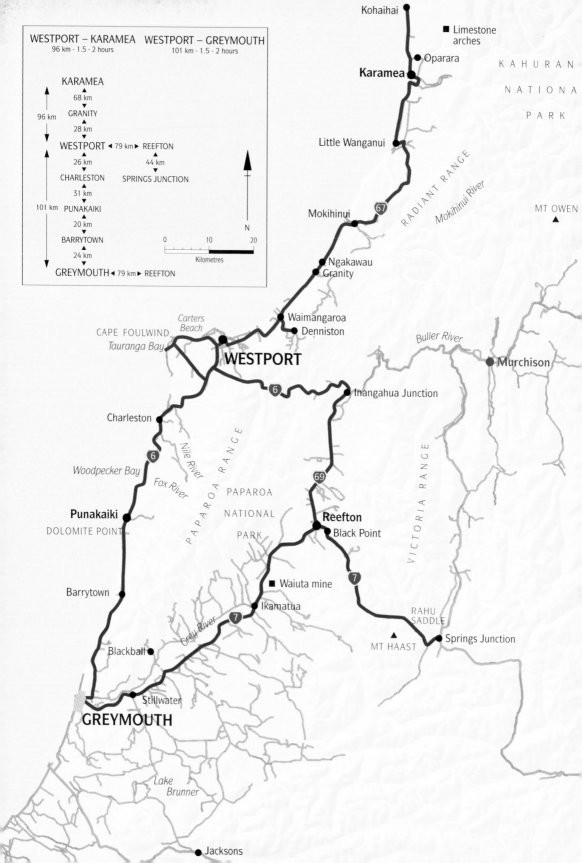

WESTPORT – KARAMEA   WESTPORT – GREYMOUTH
96 km · 1.5 - 2 hours   101 km · 1.5 - 2 hours

KARAMEA
▲
68 km
▼
GRANITY
28 km
96 km
WESTPORT ◄ 79 km ► REEFTON
26 km   44 km
CHARLESTON   SPRINGS JUNCTION
31 km
101 km PUNAKAIKI
20 km
BARRYTOWN
24 km
GREYMOUTH ◄ 79 km ► REEFTON

N

0   10   20
Kilometres

Kohaihai

■ Limestone
    arches

Oparara

Karamea

K A H U R A N
N A T I O N A
P A R K

Little Wanganui

R A D I A N T   R A N G E

Mokihinui River

MT OWEN ▲

Mokihinui

67

Ngakawau
Granity

Buller River

Waimangaroa
Denniston

● Murchison

Carters
Beach

CAPE FOULWIND
Tauranga Bay

WESTPORT

6

Inangahua Junction

Charleston

Nile River

P A P A R O A   R A N G E

V I C T O R I A   R A N G E

6

Woodpecker Bay

Fox River

PAPAROA

NATIONAL

PARK

69

Reefton
Black Point

Punakaiki

DOLOMITE POINT

7

Waiuta mine

RAHU
SADDLE

Barrytown

Grey River

Ikamatua

MT HAAST ▲

Springs Junction

7

Blackball

Stillwater

GREYMOUTH

*Lake
Brunner*

Jacksons

North Westland

Westport–Karamea SH 67
96 km, 1.5–2 hours

Though it's usually less than two hours to Karamea, you can easily spend a day pottering around historic coal-mining settlements, and enjoying walks and coastal and forest scenery along the way. Terry Sumner's *Buller Walks* (Nikau Press) is an excellent guide to this area. DoC brochures are also available.

Denniston – views, walk
Denniston is a former coal-mining town on the Denniston Plateau, 8 km above Waimangaroa. The plateau has a stark beauty and it offers fine vistas over the coast when the weather allows. Dotted around the place are mine relics and historic buildings; the Denniston Walkway between Waimangaroa and Denniston takes 3–4 hours one way.

Granity/Ngakawau – walks
After a relaxing break at Granity's Drifters Café you can drive up the hill and walk around the old Millerton township and mine. Otherwise, three kilometres from Granity at Ngakawau is the rewarding Charming Creek Walkway which follows an old railway route through river and gorge scenery.

Mokihinui – campground
SH 67 turns inland at Mokihinui on the Mokihinui River mouth. Just over the river bridge, a left turn and short drive leads to a West Coast institution – the Cow Shed Café with its adjacent accommodation complex and coastal scenery.

Karamea Bluff Ecological Reserve
The scenic highlight of the route to Karamea is the climb up the Radiant Range through the Karamea Bluff Ecological Reserve's outstanding podocarp forest, which will be ablaze with flowering rata in summer. At the base of Taffytown Hill the highway returns to coastal plains at Little Wanganui.

Karamea – campground
Karamea is the last stop before the Heaphy Track, 15 km away at Kohaihai in Kahurangi National Park. The 2 hour return walk along the Heaphy to Scotts Beach offers a taste of this beautiful forested coastline. One of New Zealand's most rewarding short walks is that to the 43 m high Oparara limestone arch in the forests of the upper Oparara Valley (turn off (signposted) 8 km from Karamea and follow the unsealed road over a steep saddle to a carpark).

Westport–Greymouth SH 6
101 km, 1.5–2 hours

The Cape Foulwind seal colony, Paparoa National Park's superb coastal scenery, and probably the only place in New Zealand where you can tuck into a buffalo meat hamburger – all within 101 km. This is another drive with enough to easily fill a day. Keep an eye out for cyclists on the narrower tracts around the coast.

Cape Foulwind seal colony – walks
The walkway to the New Zealand fur seal colony at Cape Foulwind is one of the best on the Coast. I'd recommend the 15-minute interpreted walk to the colony from the Tauranga Bay end, which is reached from Westport along SH 67a past Carters Beach and the Cape. The full walkway requires 1.5 hours one way. Back at Tauranga Bay is the superb Bay House Café. There's a direct route back to SH 6 down Wilson's Lead Road.

Charleston – campground, walks
Views of the Buckland Peaks on the northern Paparoa Range dominate the views inland towards Charleston, another West Coast mining town well past its glory days. The short walk to the Charleston sea cliffs or along the beach from the Nile River mouth are enjoyable diversions, and you can learn much about the harshness of settler life by walking round the old Charleston cemetery above the Nile River.

Dolomite Point, Punakaiki

Fox River – walks, swimming
After Charleston the road turns inland for a stretch before returning to the coast and the languorous sweep of Woodpecker Bay, where limestone cliffs loom over the beach near the Fox River at the northern boundary of Paparoa National Park. The walk up the Fox River leads to the Fox River caves (3 hours return) and canyon (5 hours). Otherwise at low tide you can explore tidal platforms toward Seal Island.

Punakaiki – campground, walks
The drive to Punakaiki, over cliffs and headlands below spectacular limestone bluffs and coastal forest, is superb. Trumans Track, 2.5 km before Punakaiki, is a highly recommended short walk at low tide by cliffs, caves and rock pools. It's hard to avoid the crush of tourists at Punakaiki if you arrive in the middle of the day in the tourist season, but the pancake rocks and blowholes at Dolomite Point in a sou'westerly swell are always exhilarating. The best coffee and food here is at Punakaiki Crafts.

Barrytown Flats – walks, buffalos
Interspersed amongst the farmland on Barrytown Flats are remnant groves of nikau palms and lush coastal forest. At Pakiroa Beach, down the road past the Barrytown pub, fossickers occasionally turn up greenstone amongst the shingle. Of the Coast's quirky attractions, none is more so than the sight of East Asian buffalos on the hill south of the pub. No ploughs or loincloth-clad farmers here – these beasts are

being fattened to be turned by the chefs at the Rata Café into steaks, burgers and casseroles. There are plenty of other eating options for the buffalo-averse.

Past Barrytown SH 6 resumes its cliff-side convolutions to Greymouth, past wind-beaten forest, glimpses up narrow canyons and hazy views over coastal headlands and the sea.

Westport–Greymouth via Reefton (Grey Valley) SH 6, 69, 7
158 km, 2.5 hours

The inland route to Greymouth traverses the eastern flanks of the Paparoa Range, down the Grey Valley from Reefton to the coast. It also connects travellers with SH 7, the quickest route between Westport and Christchurch.

The drive between Westport and Inangahua (44 km) is a wonderful drive up the lower Buller gorge with forest scenery, graceful river bends and wide shingly rapids. At Inangahua Junction, 1 km from Inangahua, go straight ahead down the Inangahua Valley (SH 69) between the Paparoa and Victoria ranges along farmed river terraces to Reefton (34 km).

Reefton – campground, walks
Highlights of a visit here are the area's historic goldmining sites, buildings and forest walks. First stop in Reefton should be at the very good Reefton Visitor Centre on Broadway. Some of the best walks are those from SH 7 between Reefton and Springs Junction (see below). Reefton's Reef Café is the pick of the cafés in this area by a long way.

Reefton–Greymouth
79 km
From Reefton SH 7 crosses Reefton Saddle and descends to the Grey Valley's south bank. An interesting side trip is to the site of the abandoned Waiuta mine and village (signposted 23 km from Reefton, 8 km unsealed, brochure and on-site interpretation). Otherwise, you might cross the Grey at Ikamatua and drive to Blackball, visit the famous historic 'Hilton' Hotel or stock up on locally made salami. Blackball is at the start of the Croesus Track across the Paparoa Range. Back on the south bank, the route to Lake Brunner and to Jacksons on SH 73 (Arthur's Pass) turns off at Stillwater. On the way to Moana is the historic Arnold River power station site (forest walks), while the Stationhouse Café at Moana on the shores of Lake Brunner offers brunch, lunch, a kids' menu and anything from muffins to gourmet burgers and a la carte dining in the evenings.

Reefton–Springs Junction to SH 7, Lewis Pass and Christchurch
44 km, 50 minutes
The main points of interest on this lovely 50-minute drive are the craggy granite tops and beech forests of Victoria Forest Park, the Blacks Point Museum and the Murray Creek walking tracks (2 km from Reefton), the Big River Track to the Golden Lead Battery (11 km from Reefton), and the track to Mt Haast (1587 m, 6 hours return) from Rahu Saddle, one of the best walks in the area in good weather. See Murchison–Christchurch (Route 42) for the drive to Christchurch from Springs Junction.

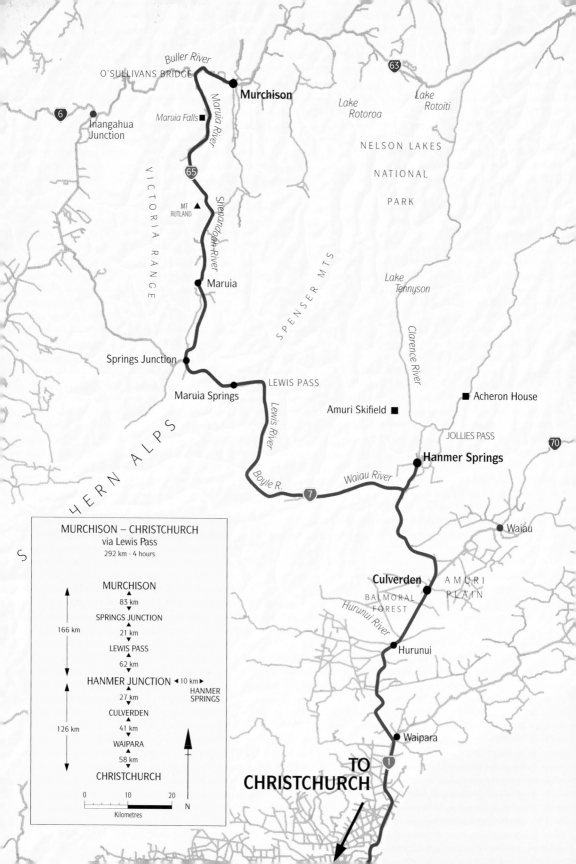

Buller River
O'SULLIVANS BRIDGE
Murchison

Maruia Falls

6
Inangahua
Junction

Maruia River

65

MT
RUTLAND

V I C T O R I A   R A N G E

Shenandoah River

Maruia

Springs Junction

Maruia Springs

LEWIS PASS

Lewis River

Boyle R.

7

S O U T H E R N   A L P S

63

Lake
Rotoroa

Lake
Rotoiti

N E L S O N   L A K E S

N A T I O N A L

P A R K

Lake
Tennyson

Clarence River

S P E N S E R   M T S

Acheron House

Amuri Skifield

JOLLIES PASS

Hanmer Springs

70

Waiau River

Waiau

Culverden

A M U R I
P L A I N

BALMORAL
FOREST

Hurunui River

Hurunui

Waipara

1

**TO
CHRISTCHURCH**

MURCHISON – CHRISTCHURCH
via Lewis Pass
292 km - 4 hours

MURCHISON
▲
83 km
▼
SPRINGS JUNCTION
▲
21 km
▼
LEWIS PASS
▲
62 km
▼
HANMER JUNCTION ◄10 km►
▲
27 km
▼   HANMER
CULVERDEN   SPRINGS
▲
41 km
▼
WAIPARA
▲
58 km
▼
CHRISTCHURCH

166 km

126 km

0   10   20
Kilometres

N

Murchison–Christchurch via Lewis Pass SH 65, 7, 1
292 km, 4 hours

Of the three crossings of the Alps (the others being Arthur's and Haast passes), the Lewis is easiest to drive thanks to the comparatively gentle approach up its western side. The first leg of this journey follows the Maruia Valley to its headwaters at Lewis Pass, with fine mountain scenery and corridors of upland beech in the Lewis Pass National Reserve. It then descends to the Waiau River to eventually emerge on the Amuri Plain near Culverden, and joins SH 1 at Waipara. Highlights of the drive are thermal resorts at Hanmer and Maruia Springs, forest walks in the reserve, and a rare opportunity to stand astride one of Planet Earth's continental plate boundaries.

Murchison

Murchison (see Nelson–Westport, Route 38 for more information) is on the Buller River which is followed for 11 km to O'Sullivans Bridge. Here, SH 6 to Westport crosses the bridge, and SH 65 continues ahead towards the confluence of the Buller and Maruia rivers. Between here and Springs Junction (allow an hour) the highway shadows the Victoria Range on the western side of the valley's farmed river flats, and ranges flanking the main Southern Alps chain to the east.

Maruia Falls – picnicking

This 9 m waterfall 22 km from Murchison was formed by the Murchison earthquake in 1929. Remarkably, the fall was originally about 1 m, but has grown 8 m as the riverbed below has lowered. The relatively safe runout has made running the falls popular with kayakers.

SH 65 continues up the Maruia Valley until a gorge section forces a deviation up the Shenandoah River and around Mt Rutland. The road narrows beyond Ruffe Creek and requires care in the forested gorge before the climb to Shenandoah Saddle. Beyond the saddle the route rejoins the Maruia, following wide farmed river flats to Springs Junction.

Springs Junction

SH 65 ends at Springs Junction where it meets SH 7 between Greymouth and Waipara (allow 45 minutes to cross Rahu Saddle to Reefton, see Westport–Greymouth, Route 41 for details). If you like white-bread sandwiches and chips with everything then the café at Springs Junction is the place for you, and some people have experienced good coffee there too.

Marble Hill Scenic Reserve – campground, picnicking

In the grassy paddock next to this innocuous little reserve, about 7 km toward Lewis Pass, the edge of the Pacific continental plate is grinding past the Indo-Australasian plate, forcing the Southern Alps skywards and skewing the West Coast northwards. Honest! This boundary, also called the Alpine Fault, runs up the western side of the Alps from Milford Sound to Nelson Lakes. Here at Marble Hill the scene of the action is a boggy terrace running across the paddock where in 1964 geologists placed a concrete wall at right angles to the fault to measure any movement. On the upper side of the terrace is the Pacific

Plate, on the lower side the Indo-Australasian. It is rare in the world to find an exact and active surface expression of a major plate boundary. It may distress some to learn that Richter 8 earthquakes along the Alpine Fault are believed to have occurred every 300 years, and one of these is well overdue. On the plus side, proximity to the fault is responsible for the thermal springs that lie ahead.

Maruia Springs – walks
From Marble Hill the road winds through beech forest next to the gravelly upper reaches of the Maruia River. About 2 km before Maruia Springs is the easy Waterfall Track (20 minutes return). Maruia Springs resort (98 km from Murchison) has public and private pools – the hot water is piped from the springs on the north bank of the river.

Maruia Springs

Lewis Pass – walks, picnicking, views
Lewis Pass is about 6 km beyond the resort after a steep climb through forest with views north toward Gloriana Peak. Just below the pass on the Canterbury side is a carpark at the start of the St James Walkway, a nice picnic spot amid alpine scenery and forests. There is a nature trail around the nearby alpine wetland, or a longer walk down to the picturesque Cannibal Gorge (2 hours return), where centuries ago Ngai Tahu warriors were said to have overwhelmed a party of Ngati Wairangi, and killed and eaten them – but don't let that put you off your lunch.

Lewis Pass–Hanmer Springs

The turnoff to Hanmer Springs is 62 km from Lewis Pass, the first 20 km of which follows the Lewis River south through corridors of beech toward the Boyle River (where the highway turns east). Now on open and scrubby farmed river terraces flanked by high ranges, the road crosses to the southern bank of the river and joins the larger braided Waiau River, generally staying high above it until the junction with SH 7a.

Hanmer Springs – campground, walks

Hanmer Springs is an alpine spa town which has been frequented by tourists since the 1860s. The main attraction, the town's outdoor thermal reserve, administered by the Department of Conservation, is a lovely place for a soothing soak. Hanmer has a range of cafés and bars – try the Springs Deli Café for food, and The Powerhouse Café for the best coffee. There are many short walks in the Hanmer Forest, which is predominantly comprised of introduced conifers – forest trails are also popular with mountain-bikers. In winter the Amuri Skifield adds another attraction to the town's list of outdoor activities. The drive up Jollies Pass (unsealed) takes you to the edge of the high country between Hanmer and Blenheim. Acheron Accommodation House, a cob cottage built in the 1860s, now a registered historic place, is a short distance from the pass in the Clarence Valley. For several weeks during January and February each year it's possible to drive through Molesworth Station to the Awatere Valley south of Blenheim (see Picton–Christchurch, Route 45 for details).

Culverden/Hurunui – campground

From Hanmer Springs SH 7 continues along the Waiau Valley through rolling hills to emerge on the Amuri Plain. Here the highway leaves the river and turns south toward Culverden. SH 70 to Waiau and the inland route to Kaikoura turns off just before Culverden (see Picton–Christchurch, Route 45). If you've skipped Hanmer you can get good quality café fare at Culverden's Legacy Garden Café across the road from the store. Otherwise there's the historic Hurunui Hotel 13 km further past the Balmoral pine plantation (campground), just over the Hurunui River. Waipara and the SH 1 junction is 28 km away. See Route 45 for information on cafés between Waipara and Christchurch.

Highway near Springs Junction

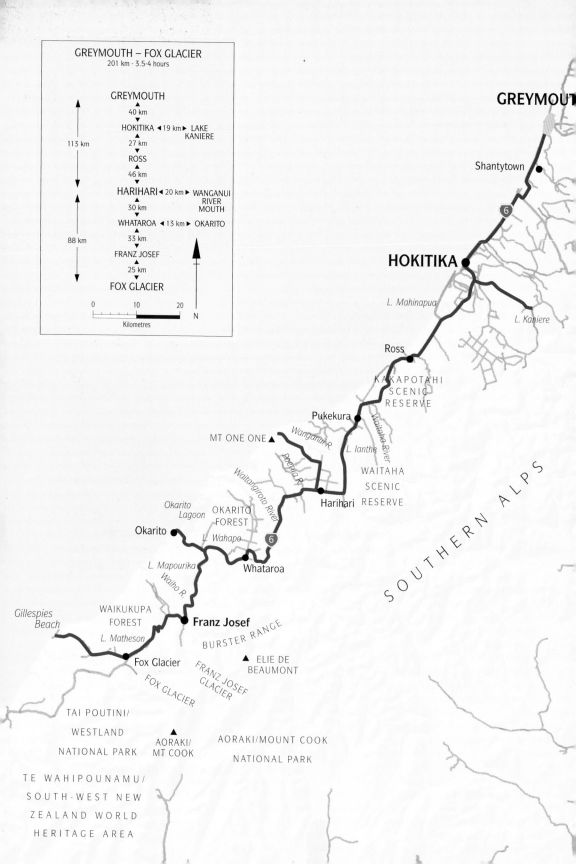

GREYMOUTH – FOX GLACIER
201 km - 3.5-4 hours

GREYMOUTH ▲
40 km ▼
HOKITIKA ◄ 19 km ► LAKE
▲ KANIERE
27 km ▼
ROSS ▲
46 km ▼
HARIHARI ◄ 20 km ► WANGANUI
▲ RIVER
30 km ▼ MOUTH
WHATAROA ◄ 13 km ► OKARITO
33 km ▼
FRANZ JOSEF ▲
25 km ▼
FOX GLACIER

113 km

88 km

0   10   20
Kilometres

N

GREYMOUT

Shantytown

6

HOKITIKA

L. Mahinapua

L. Kaniere

Ross

KAKAPOTAHI
SCENIC
RESERVE

Pukekura

Waitaha River

Wanganui R.

L. Ianthe

WAITAHA
SCENIC
RESERVE

MT ONE ONE ▲

Poerua R.

Waitangiroto River

Harihari

Okarito
Lagoon

OKARITO
FOREST

Okarito

L. Wahapo

6

Whataroa

L. Mapourika

Waiho R.

SOUTHERN ALPS

Gillespies
Beach

WAIKUKUPA
FOREST

L. Matheson

Franz Josef

BURSTER RANGE

Fox Glacier

FRANZ JOSEF
GLACIER

FOX GLACIER

ELIE DE ▲
BEAUMONT

TAI POUTINI/

WESTLAND

NATIONAL PARK

AORAKI/ ▲
MT COOK

AORAKI/MOUNT COOK

NATIONAL PARK

TE WAHIPOUNAMU/

SOUTH-WEST NEW

ZEALAND WORLD

HERITAGE AREA

Greymouth–Fox Glacier SH 6
201 km, 3.5–4 hours

Much of this memorable journey into South Westland is within sight of the high peaks of the Southern Alps. Even when it's wet (and it does rain at times!), the wild coastline, rainforests, lakes, rivers and glaciated landscapes are no less extraordinary. By Whataroa you will have entered Tai Poutini/Westland National Park and the northern reaches of the vast Te Wahipounamu South-West New Zealand World Heritage Area. Some words of advice: take insect repellent and buy fuel at Greymouth or Hokitika – prices at places like Whataroa and Franz Josef amount to daylight robbery. West Coast wild food – including whitebait and venison – are specialities worth looking out for in the region's cafés, and every March Hokitika hosts the famous 'Wild Foods Festival'.

Greymouth – campground, walks

Greymouth, a good place to gather information about the journey south, is not short of attractions itself. They include quality coffee and home-cooked food from the Smelting House Café on MacKay Street; and Shantytown, a model nineteenth-century mining village 13 km south of the town. Greymouth has a number of short forest walks within the borough – covered by a DoC brochure. On dolphin-watching boat cruises, you're likely to see fur seals and coastal birds as well as the critically endangered Hector's dolphin.

Hokitika – campground, walks, picnicking, swimming, boating

Hokitika is about 30 minutes south of Greymouth and 15 minutes from the SH 73 junction (Arthur's Pass and Christchurch). The town's attractions include its jade/craft galleries and one of the Coast's best museums. Café de Paris and PR's Café are the pick of the cafés, along with Café Priya for those after a decent curry. 19 km east of Hokitika is Lake Kaniere where an easy track along its western shores leads through the beautiful podocarp forest that lines the lake's tranquil bays. The full walk requires 4 hours one way, but shorter walks are no less rewarding. Lake Mahinapua is 10 km south of Hokitika on SH 6. There are several short walks and the 2 hour (one way) Mahinapua Walkway, but it's pleasant enough just to fetch up on the lakeshore for a picnic or to camp.

Ross – walks, picnicking

Ross is the centre of the Ross Historic Goldfields, and trails like the water-race walk radiate away from the visitor centre on Aylmer Street. The pride of Ross, which no-one dares criticise within earshot of the locals, is its not-so-historic opencast gold mine a few metres behind the visitor centre – the largest opencast alluvial mine in the Southern Hemisphere.

Pukekura/Lake Ianthe – campground, picnicking, walks

South of Ross, the highway traverses corridors of rimu and matai forest in the Kakapotahi and Waitaha Scenic Reserves. Up the hill from the Waitaha River bridge at Pukekura is the Puke Pub and Wild Food Restaurant, which boasts possum pie and other local delicacies on its menu. Across the road is the quaint

'Bushman's Centre' dedicated to the bushman's arts. Lake Ianthe is a large forest-fringed glacial lake, popular with swimmers, campers and anglers. Natural history tours of the lake by boat leave every half hour.

Harihari – campground, walks, picnicking

From Lake Ianthe SH 6 turns inland toward the foothills of the Southern Alps. The 20 km side trip from Harihari to the Wanganui River mouth leads to one of the lesser-known gems on the coast – the 45-minute walk to the Mt One One (Doughboy) lookout where superb views unfold across unbroken forest to the Alps. You can continue along the coast on the Harihari Coastal Walk to the Poerua River mouth. The Mt One One–Poerua circuit (3 hours) is described in a brochure available at Harihari.

Whataroa

Turn left at the Whataroa Bridge to the 'Tourist Recreation Area' for an inexpensive venison or whitebait burger, a free cup of smoky billy tea and a chance to go gold panning. Tours of the white heron colony at Whataroa's Waitangiroto Lagoon are the major attraction. The prominent peak seen from several places between Whataroa and Franz Josef is Elie de Beaumont (3109 m).

Southern Alps from Lake Mapourika

Okarito Lagoon – walks, picnicking

A couple of kilometres past Lake Wahapo is the 13 km road to Okarito, a small community of baches and homes on a magnificent stretch of coast bordering Tai Poutini/Westland National Park. Okarito's rimu forests are a symbol of the successful battle against loggers in the 1980s – their addition to the national park has protected intact a sequence of ecosystems from coast to mountains – rare not just in New Zealand but in the world. Since then it's been learned that the Okarito brown kiwi is a distinct sub-species – recent government funding has established a kiwi sanctuary here. On a fine day the view from Okarito Trig (1.5 hours return) across Okarito Forest to the high peaks of the national park is incomparable. Bird-watching by hired canoe on Okarito Lagoon and beach walks are other popular activities.

Lake Mapourika – campground, fishing, picnicking, boating, swimming

Lake Mapourika, 11 km from Franz Josef is the largest and most scenic of South Westland's glacial lakes. Like the much larger 'great lakes' east of the Alps, these lakes were created as glaciers retreated when the last Ice Age waned 10,000–13,000 years ago.

Franz Josef – campground, walks

Franz Josef Glacier has been a tourist icon since the late nineteenth century, and they come still in ever increasing numbers to see it. Take your hat, coat and sensible shoes (and earplugs if you're averse to

Sheep grazing near Fox Glacier with Mt Tasman and Aoraki/Mt Cook behind

aircraft noise) for the walk to the base of the glacier (1.5 hours return), which begins up the Waiho Valley just south of the village. Be especially careful not to go too close to the unstable terminal face of the glacier. A roadend kiosk within sight of the glacier has an informative series of interpretive panels on glacier formation and the story of the Franz. Guided walks onto the glacier can be arranged at the village. Other high quality shorter walks in the valley include those to Peters Pool, Lake Wombat and to Sentinel Rock – the latter offering good views of the glacier. Information on these walks is found at the DoC visitor centre at the Tai Poutini/Westland National Park headquarters.

Fox Glacier – campground, walks

The 25-minute drive to Fox Glacier covers steep forested terrain as it crosses Cook Saddle. Fox Glacier village isn't as developed as Franz Josef, though even that status is changing rapidly. For walkers, access to the glacier is easier and quicker (1 hour return) than the Franz, and it benefits too from the long established company Alpine Guides Westland whose guides and guided walks enjoy a good reputation. The Fox Glacier terminal is no less dangerous than the Franz. Fox's most regarded walk is the easy circuit through the forests around Lake Matheson (reached off Cook Flat Road toward the coast), famous for its reflections of the Southern Alps at dawn and dusk. When evening light colours the mountains, Gillespies Beach, 19 km from Fox Glacier through Waikukupa Forest (unsealed), is a wonderful place to be.

Walkers on the terminal of the Fox Glacier

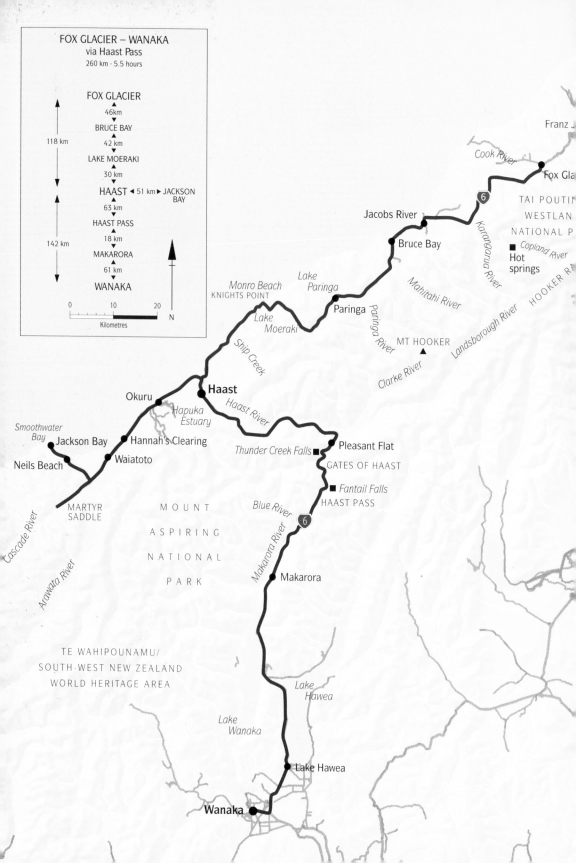

FOX GLACIER – WANAKA
via Haast Pass
260 km - 5.5 hours

FOX GLACIER
▲ 46km ▼
BRUCE BAY
▲ 42km ▼
LAKE MOERAKI
▲ 30km ▼
HAAST ◄ 51 km ► JACKSON BAY
▲ 63km ▼
HAAST PASS
▲ 18km ▼
MAKARORA
▲ 61km ▼
WANAKA

118 km

142 km

0   10   20
Kilometres

N

Franz J

Cook River

Fox Gla

6

TAI POUTIN
WESTLAN
NATIONAL P

Jacobs River

Karangarua River

Copland River
■ Hot
springs

HOOKER RA

Bruce Bay

Mahitahi River

Monro Beach
KNIGHTS POINT

Lake
Paringa

Paringa

Paringa River

MT HOOKER ▲

Landsborough River

Lake
Moeraki

Ship Creek

Clarke River

Haast

Haast River

Okuru

Hapuka
Estuary

Thunder Creek Falls ■

Pleasant Flat

GATES OF HAAST

Smoothwater
Bay

Jackson Bay

Hannah's Clearing

Waiatoto

■ Fantail Falls
HAAST PASS

Neils Beach

Blue River

6

Cascade River

MARTYR
SADDLE

Makarora River

M O U N T

A S P I R I N G

Makarora

Arawata River

N A T I O N A L

P A R K

Lake
Hawea

TE WAHIPOUNAMU/
SOUTH-WEST NEW ZEALAND
WORLD HERITAGE AREA

Lake
Wanaka

Lake Hawea

Wanaka

Fox Glacier–Wanaka via Haast Pass SH 6
260 km, 5.5 hours

The drive between Fox Glacier and Wanaka is dominated by the coastal, forest and mountain landscapes that form the central portion of the Te Wahipounamu South-West New Zealand World Heritage Area. From Haast, the road jags inland for the crossing of Haast Pass to Otago's gentler, beech-forested landscape and the shores of Lake Wanaka. Highlights of the route are the many short walks to a variety of coastal and forest features, perfect for the traveller. Although described as a southward journey below, the best experience of it in my opinion is travelling northwards from Wanaka, leaving around 2 p.m. and driving as the late afternoon and evening sun lights the high peaks and forests between Haast and Fox.

Fox Glacier–Bruce Bay – walks, picnicking
The 46 km drive to Bruce Bay crosses the coastal plains formed by the Cook and Karangarua rivers. Single-lane suspension bridges carry you across these two large fast-flowing rivers – the latter, 30 minutes from Fox, provides access to the Copland Track to Welcome Flat Hut and its nearby hot springs (6–8 hours one way). Bruce Bay, littered with driftwood and lined to the north by rimu forest and ranks of flax, marks a brief return to the coast before the highway again enters forests up the Mahitahi River. Views inland from here reach toward the remote peaks and snowfields of the Hooker-Landsborough Wilderness Area.

Paringa – campground, picnicking
The route between Bruce Bay and Lake Moeraki stays inland, wending through tall dark South Westland forests much of the way. At the Paringa River the route opens briefly onto river plains. On the northern bank is the Salmon Farm Café, while a little further on at Lake Paringa is the recommended Heritage Lodge Café. Lake Paringa is enclosed by forest and is a popular swimming, camping and picnicking area. Access to the lake is a short distance from the café.

Lake Moeraki/Monro Beach – walks, picnicking
Just past Lake Moeraki and close to the Lake Moeraki Wilderness Lodge is the forest track to Monro Beach and the Whakapohai Wildlife Refuge (40 minutes one way). The refuge protects breeding areas used by tawaki (Fiordland crested penguin) between July and December.

Knights Point lookout/ Ship Creek – views, picnicking, walks
4 km past Lake Moeraki SH 6 reaches the spectacular coastline north of Haast at Knights Point. After winding around steep headlands and gullies, the road returns to forested coastal plains and a series of dune ridges. At Ship Creek is an excellent 20-minute kahikatea swamp forest walk – primeval scenery which has made photographers and film-

Bruce Bay

makers wealthy and is the delight of ecologists who regard this area's forests as the best representation anywhere of the Mesozoic-era swamp forests that existed 100 million years ago. Ship Creek's 30-minute Dune Lake circuit through wind-stunted forest offers fine views over lake and coastline.

Haast

Haast is heralded by the crossing of the wide and braided Haast River. Inside the Haast Visitor Centre is information on the World Heritage Area and brochures on the walks noted in this section. Haast is the last place for fuel until Makarora (81 km) on the Otago side of Haast Pass. There are a couple of cafés at Haast township, including one at the McGuire Lodge. See below for the Haast–Jacksons Bay description.

Haast River

The way to Haast Pass follows the Haast River to its headwaters, probably the most dramatic of any of the road crossings of the Alps. SH 6 traces the south bank of the river beneath alpine tops and steep forested valley walls on the boundary of Mount Aspiring National Park. Where the Landsborough River joins the Haast, about 40 km from the coast, the Haast River and SH 6 make an abrupt turn south.

Pleasant Flat – campground, picnicking

Located a few kilometres from the Haast-Landsborough confluence, on a fine day Pleasant Flat is indeed pleasant. Vistas spread north up the Landsborough and Clarke valleys to the impressive southern face of Mt Hooker and peaks of the Hooker Range – the centrepiece of the Hooker/Landsborough Wilderness Area.

Gates of Haast – views, walks

Next to the flat, the highway crosses the Haast River and enters Mount Aspiring National Park and the breathtaking Gates of Haast, a narrow and dramatic gorge where slips and enormous boulders choke the river's passage. It is hard to imagine that the easy flowing river a few kilometres on is the source of this imbroglio that cuts steeply down toward the coast. After a second crossing of the river are two short and rewarding forest walks to Thunder Creek and Fantail Falls.

Haast Pass (563 m)

West of the pass the forests are dominated by kamahi, but on the pass itself, atop a gentle rise above the headwaters of the Haast River, silver beech is the most common tree. The Haast is the lowest of the three Southern Alps passes, and, as an interpretive panel notes, it was a well-known route used by Maori. The pass was first reached by a European explorer, J.H. Baker, in 1861 but was then controversially named after Julius von Haast who crossed it to the West Coast in 1863. A packhorse trail over the pass was established by the 1870s, but construction of the highway between Hawea and Haast was spread across no less than 36 years between 1929 and 1965!

Haast Pass–Makarora – campground, walks, picnicking

From the pass you are soon into gentler topography at the head of the Makarora Valley. Towards Lake Wanaka the highway follows the bed of the steadily broadening valley formed by one of many gargantuan glaciers that flowed through the area during the Pleistocene Ice Age. There are camping/picnic sites and walks at Cameron and Davis flats, and a 30-minute walk to beautiful river pools at the mouth of the Blue River. At Makarora there is a DoC visitor centre, campground, store and café.

Lakes Wanaka & Hawea

Most of the 61 km drive between Makarora and Wanaka is high above these impressive glacier-formed lakes. There are a number of lookouts and picnicking sites where you can enjoy lake and mountain scenery, including the camping area at Boundary Creek. See Christchurch–Wanaka (Route 51) for information about services at Wanaka.

Haast–Jackson Bay
51 km, 45 minutes

The short stretch of highway to Jackson Bay, along the coastal strip west of Mount Aspiring National Park, leads to remote beaches and rivers as well as forest and mountain scenery and several interesting walks.

Hapuka Estuary Walk – walk

Just past Okuru is this easy 20-minute walk through coastal forest and the Hapuka Estuary intertidal zone. It is one of those rare places (in the world) where wetlands are given due for the important ecological role they play. Forest and coastal birds are likely to be seen, while information panels provide natural history interpretation.

Rainforest, South Westland

Jackson Bay – walks

From Hannah's Clearing the road enters a beautiful corridor of forest, emerging briefly where it crosses the Waiatoto and enters the Haast tokoeka sanctuary. At the legendary Arawata River the sealed route turns west to Neils Beach where a bumpy sandy road leads to the Arawata mouth, and a wild beach – watch for penguins! At Jackson Bay a DoC shelter and information kiosk opposite the wharf describes both the natural and cultural history of the Bay, and you can enjoy great takeaways at The Craypot. Walks from here lead to Wharekai Te Kau wildlife refuge (20 minutes, information panels) and Smoothwater Bay (3–4 hours return).

Red Hills Lookout – views

A 22 km unsealed route from just past the Arawata River bridge leads to a lookout over the Cascade River and rugged surrounding hinterland. A lookout (with natural history information panels) 3 km past Martyr Saddle offers views south over the valley toward the Red Hills – a region of outstanding natural and wilderness values.

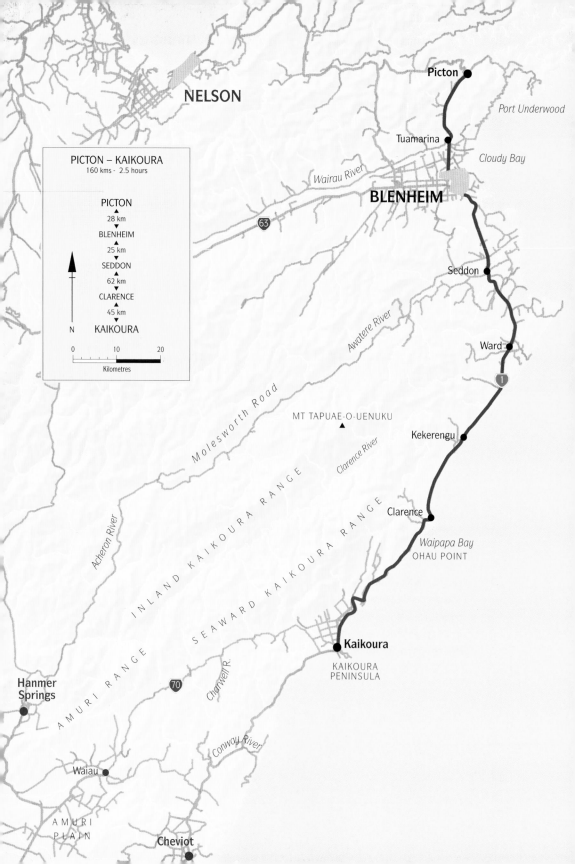

NELSON

PICTON

Tuamarina

Port Underwood

Cloudy Bay

Wairau River

BLENHEIM

63

Seddon

Awatere River

Ward

1

MT TAPUAE-O-UENUKU ▲

Kekerengu

Clarence River

Molesworth Road

Clarence

Waipapa Bay
OHAU POINT

Acheron River

INLAND KAIKOURA RANGE

SEAWARD KAIKOURA RANGE

Kaikoura

KAIKOURA
PENINSULA

Hanmer
Springs

AMURI RANGE

70

Charwell R.

Conway River

Waiau

AMURI
PLAIN

Cheviot

PICTON – KAIKOURA
160 kms - 2.5 hours

PICTON
▲
28 km
▼
BLENHEIM
▲
25 km
▼
SEDDON
▲
62 km
▼
CLARENCE
▲
45 km
▼
KAIKOURA

N

0   10   20
Kilometres

Picton–Christchurch SH 1
346 km, 5 hours

SH 1 is the busy main route south to Christchurch. Beginning in Marlborough's world-class wine-growing region, SH 1 passes to Kaikoura's famed whale, dolphin and seal-watching coast before crossing to the Canterbury Plains.

Picton–Kaikoura, 160 km, 2.5 hours

Picton – campground
The Picton Visitor Centre, on the waterfront a few hundred metres from the ferry terminal, is a useful place to collect information on the places ahead. For a bite to eat try Cibo or Café Zest on High Street.

Blenheim – campground
Blenheim was one of New Zealand's earliest settlements, its current prosperity founded on the region's suitability for sheep farming and horticulture. These days its fame as a winegrowing region has encouraged an attractive café, wine and craft-trail culture (see also Picton–Nelson, Route 35) that draws people from all over the globe. (Take SH 63 up the Wairau Valley to reach St Arnaud and Nelson Lakes National Park – 127 km, 1.5 hours.)

Seddon/Ward – campground, views
Just south of Blenheim is the large Montana winery, after which SH 1 crosses Dashwood Pass to Seddon in the Awatere Valley. From here the vistas west are filled by the foothills rising toward Mt Tapuae-o-Uenuku (2885 m) and its outriders on the Inland Kaikoura Range. (See also the Molesworth Road description below.) Seddon has a couple of cafés including the Oak Tree Cottage tea and coffee shop at the Vavasour winery (turn towards the coast at the Awatere Valley Road intersection before the road/rail bridge).

Kekerengu & Kaikoura Coast – campground
The first leg of the Kaikoura coast highway to Clarence River lies between steep hillsides and a 30 km shingle beach. Halfway down the beach at Kekerengu is 'The Store' (named after its humble predecessor), a fine café, craft shop and gardens. Best of all is the uninterrupted sea view from the porch while you're enjoying coffee and cake.

At the Clarence River you're confronted by the eastern wall of the Seaward Kaikoura Range, which rises an incredible 2500 m in just 12 km from the sea – a faster rise than most of the Southern Alps. Further inland are the southeastern faces of the Inland Kaikoura peaks. Past Maungamanu Bay on a big turn inland stands the newish Hapuku Café with an all day breakfast and seafood specialities. Freshly cooked crayfish are sold from roadside caravans on the rocky coast at the base of the range. There's a DoC campground at Waipapa Bay, and a lookout over the Ohau Point seal colony which is well worth stopping to view.

Kaikoura – campground, walks, marine mammal watching

Kai means food, koura means crayfish; however it's watching ocean mammals that has transformed Kaikoura from crayfishing port to tourist mecca. Once you've recovered your land legs, and enjoyed lunch at one of Kaikoura's many cafés (Hislop's for organic tucker), make the circuit or a shorter walk on Kaikoura Peninsula with its seal colonies, birdlife, and great views of the Kaikoura mountains and coast.

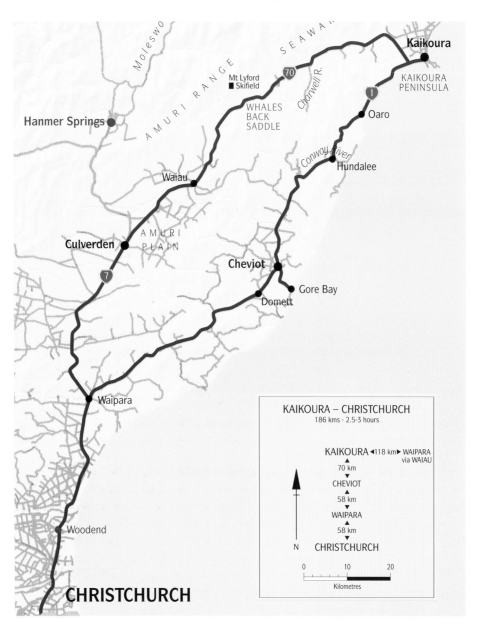

Kaikoura

KAIKOURA PENINSULA

Mt Lyford Skifield

WHALES BACK SADDLE

Oaro

Hanmer Springs

AMURI RANGE

Molesworth

SEAWARD

Chalwell R.

Conway River

Hundalee

Waiau

AMURI PLAIN

Culverden

Cheviot

Gore Bay

Domett

Waipara

Woodend

CHRISTCHURCH

KAIKOURA – CHRISTCHURCH
186 kms - 2.5-3 hours

KAIKOURA ◄118 km► WAIPARA
via WAIAU
▲
70 km
▼
CHEVIOT
▲
58 km
▼
WAIPARA
▲
58 km
▼
CHRISTCHURCH

N

0   10   20
Kilometres

DoC has done a good job with the displays and information on Kaikoura's natural and human history at the town's visitor centre on the waterfront.

Kaikoura–Waipara via Waiau SH 70, 7
118 km, 2 hours

This is a scenic alternate route to Waipara with fine views of the Seaward Kaikoura and Amuri ranges and back towards Mt Tapuae-o-Uenuku. SH 70 strikes inland 4 km south of Kaikoura, and contrary to current maps the road is now entirely sealed. Mt Lyford Lodge at the turnoff to Mt Lyford skifield has a good restaurant catering for passing travellers.

 Waiau is a sleepy village with a store, garage and a couple of pubs. The Ramshead Café and Bar (more bar than café) makes nice scones but head for Hanmer or to Culverden's Legacy Gardens Café for a break. SH 7 is 19 km from Waiau, and Hanmer Springs 52 km.

Kaikoura–Waipara SH 1
70 km, 1 hour

 Cheviot – picnicking

South of Kaikoura at Oaro the road climbs through rural hill country as it crosses the Hundalee Hills to the Conway River. Gore Bay, 15 minutes east of Cheviot, is a popular surf beach with safe swimming, picnic sites and a campground. There's no shop. Cheviot has a couple of tearooms, but the best food and coffee hereabouts is 6 km further south at Domett's Mainline Station café – a converted railway station.

 Waipara

SH 1 descends to the Canterbury Plains down the Greta Valley. Waipara is at the junction with SH 7 from Lewis Pass and Hanmer Springs. Several wineries have opened cafés here, while every Sunday from January to the end of March the Weka Pass steam train excursion departs at 11.30 a.m. and 2 p.m. (for the remainder of the year the train runs on the first and third Sundays of the month).

Allow 45 minutes to an hour to reach central Christchurch from Waipara. Two excellent cafés are worth noting – Amberley's Nor'wester Café, and the Pukeko Junction Café just south of Leithfield. Those travelling to Arthur's Pass can turn off at Woodend and travel via Oxford to reach SH 73 at Waddington (58 km). (See Woodend–Geraldine, Route 47.)

Molesworth Road

The Molesworth Road between the Awatere Valley (south of Blenheim) and Hanmer Springs is opened each summer for a limited season by the Department of Conservation, usually between New Year and early February. Molesworth Road crosses historic Molesworth Station, a large inland Marlborough sheep and cattle station (now part of a conservation area managed by DoC); the area's dry-country landscapes are often stunning, especially in the upper Awatere Valley as it rounds the Inland Kaikoura Range, and in the Acheron Valley. Between the upper Awatere and Hanmer Springs the road is unsealed but usually passable to all vehicles. There are no facilities and travellers are advised to be well-prepared for breakdowns, flat tyres etc. There is a fee to use the road. Camping is possible at each end, but not within the station itself. The road is closed during high fire risk periods or bad weather. A brochure about the route is available from visitor centres.

Banks Peninsula
Christchurch–Akaroa via Port Hills & SH 75
97 km, 1.5 hours
This rewarding scenic route to Akaroa on Banks Peninsula begins on the Summit Road on Christchurch's Port Hills. The return journey can be made via the peninsula's remote harbours and bays on its northern coastline – in total an enjoyable day excursion from Christchurch.

Summit Road
Drive to Sumner village and take the road to Evans Pass. A right turn at the pass puts you on the Summit Road, which follows the crest of the Port Hills to Gebbies Pass (1 hour). Exceptional views across Lyttelton Harbour and the Canterbury Plains can be experienced from a number of walks and viewpoints en route. The road is narrow and must be shared with cyclists, runners and walkers.

Little River

SH 75 is joined below Gebbies Pass at the Palmdale Café. The highway skirts the shallow Lake Ellesmere and turns northeast towards Lake Forsyth and Little River village. Little River Café offers great coffee and lunches.

Barrys Bay/Duvauchelle – campground, swimming, fishing

From Little River the road climbs to a saddle below French Hill with views over Akaroa Harbour from the Hilltop Tavern. Cabbage trees line the harbour at Barrys Bay where you can buy locally made cheeses or drive 3 km around the west side of the harbour to French Farm winery. The Hotel des Pecheurs at Duvauchelle is the first intimation of the Peninsula's Gallic influence. Just down the road the French ensign flies over the old Post and Telegraph office, now a stylish café with views down the harbour.

Akaroa – campground, swimming, fishing, marine mammals

Historic homes nestle amid the new at Akaroa which markets its French heritage to the hilt. European architecture, cafés, wine bars, galleries and craft shops lend a relaxed Mediterranean air to the settlement. On the beach on Rue Jolie is the excellent Waterfront Eaterie.

A recommended return journey to Christchurch is along the summit road above Akaroa back to the saddle at the Hilltop Tavern. From Akaroa take Long Bay Road (past Akaroa Winery and Café) and turn left onto the summit road. As well as offering fine views, the road provides access to Le Bons, Okains, Little Akaloa and Pigeon bays. There's a serviced motor camp at Le Bons Bay, and a museum, shop and fuel at Okains.

Lyttelton–Diamond Harbour/Purau Bay/Port Levy – swimming, campgrounds

This route rounds Lyttelton Harbour (café at Governors Bay), passes Charteris Bay (good swimming beach) to reach Diamond Harbour (Godley House Café and gardens). A sealed road (narrow and windy) continues to Purau Bay (swimming beach) and on to Port Levy (12 km from Diamond Harbour).

Banks Peninsula

Oxford

Rangiora

Springfield

Woodend

Waddington

MT HUTT

Glentunnel

Windwhistle

RAKAIA GORGE

CHRISTCHURCH

ALFORD
FOREST

Alford Forest

Methven

Rakaia River

PEEL
FOREST

Arundel

Rangitata River

Geraldine

Rangitata

79

Winchester

Washdyke

WOODEND – GERALDINE
179 km - 2.5 hours

WOODEND
▲
39 km
▼
OXFORD
▲
19 km
▼
WADDINGTON
▲
44 km
▼
MOUNT HUTT STATION ◄13 km►
METHVEN
▲
12 km
▼
ALFORD FOREST
▲
51 km
▼
ARUNDEL ◄12 km► PEEL FOREST
▲
14 km
▼
GERALDINE

N

0   10   20
Kilometres

Woodend–Geraldine SH 72
179 km, 2.5 hours

SH 72, the 'Inland Scenic Route', bypasses Christchurch on a route tracing the western edge of the Canterbury Plains. It's also a convenient bypass to SH 73 (Arthur's Pass) for those travelling from Picton, and a less busy route to Mount Cook. Highlights are the Rakaia Gorge, Mt Hutt and the Peel and Alford forests.

Woodend–SH 73 Junction at Waddington
Like much of this route, the 30-minute drive to Waddington via Rangiora and Oxford townships traverses the flat expanses of the Canterbury Plains. At the SH 73 junction at Waddington, turn east down SH 73 for about 1 km to return to the Inland Scenic Route.

Rakaia Gorge – campground, walks, fishing
The countryside hereabouts is a mix of sheep farms, forests and market gardens set against the backdrop of rising hills towards Mt Hutt. Glentunnel and Windwhistle are quiet country localities each with a store and a garage. Not far from Windwhistle the route drops sharply into the Rakaia Valley just below the Rakaia Gorge. Jetboating and salmon fishing on this large glacial river are popular activities, as is walking the gorge walkway (3–4 hours return).

Mt Hutt/Methven – skiing
The turnoff to Mt Hutt Skifield is 7 km from Mt Hutt Station (the skifield road is closed in summer). Methven, a 13 km detour off SH 72, has a good information centre, and a number of cafés.

Stavely/Alford Forest – walks, picnicking
New owners of the Stavely store have answered the call for a traveller's café on this route so stop in for snacks and tea and coffee. Alford Forest, about 4 km northwest of Stavely, has a number of recommended walks, including the excellent Sub-alpine Walkway.

Peel Forest – campground, walks, picnicking, fishing
This 550 ha native forest reserve close to the Rangitata River is a popular holiday location 12 km north of Arundel.

Geraldine – campground
Geraldine is a pleasant mid-Canterbury town, and a waypoint for those travelling to Mount Cook or further south. I can recommend the delights of the Berry Barn bakery on the main street, while across the street is the award-winning Riverside Café. Other Geraldine highlights include specialty chocolates and great coffee at Chocolate Fellman, a vintage car museum and several easy walking trails.

From Geraldine, drive south 11 km to Winchester to rejoin SH 1. If travelling to Mount Cook and the Mackenzie Country, take SH 79 to Fairlie (46 km, 45 minutes) and join SH 8 from Washdyke (see Christchurch–Wanaka, Route 51).

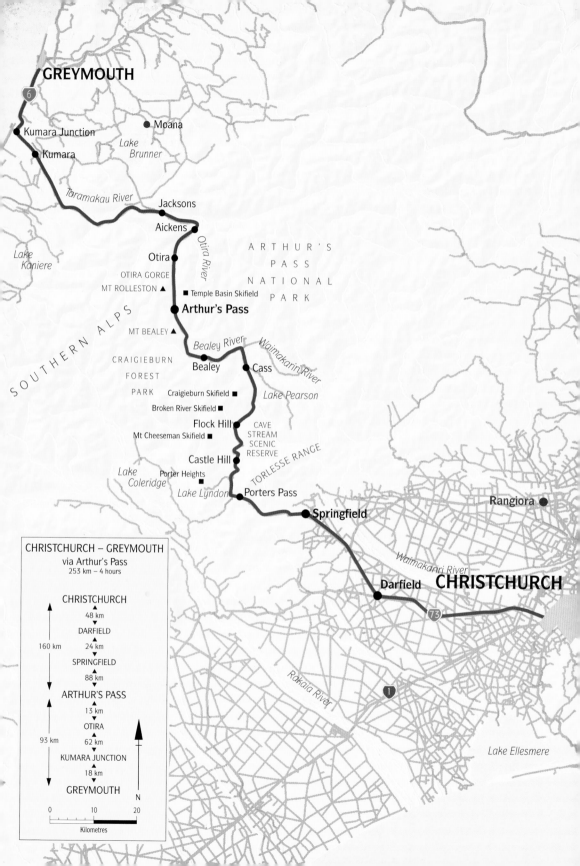

GREYMOUTH

6

Kumara Junction

Moana

Kumara

Lake Brunner

Taramakau River

Jacksons

Aickens

Lake Kaniere

Otira

Otira River

A R T H U R ' S
P A S S
N A T I O N A L
P A R K

OTIRA GORGE

MT ROLLESTON ▲   ■ Temple Basin Skifield

Arthur's Pass

MT BEALEY ▲

Bealey River

Waimakariri River

S O U T H E R N   A L P S

CRAIGIEBURN

FOREST

PARK

Bealey

Cass

Craigieburn Skifield ■

Lake Pearson

Broken River Skifield ■

Mt Cheeseman Skifield ■

Flock Hill

CAVE
STREAM
SCENIC
RESERVE

Castle Hill

Lake Coleridge

Porter Heights
■

Lake Lyndon

Porters Pass

T O R L E S S E   R A N G E

Springfield

Rangiora

Waimakariri River

Darfield   CHRISTCHURCH

73

Rakaia River

1

Lake Ellesmere

CHRISTCHURCH – GREYMOUTH
via Arthur's Pass
253 km – 4 hours

CHRISTCHURCH
▲
48 km
▼
DARFIELD
▲
24 km
▼
160 km
SPRINGFIELD
▲
88 km
▼
ARTHUR'S PASS
▲
13 km
▼
OTIRA
▲
62 km
93 km
▼
KUMARA JUNCTION
▲
18 km
▼
GREYMOUTH

N

0   10   20
Kilometres

Christchurch–Greymouth via Arthur's Pass SH 73, 6
253 km, 4 hours

This superb route across the Southern Alps over Arthur's Pass was opened in 1866 – an astonishing feat given the rugged terrain early roadbuilders had to contend with, especially on the western approach up the Otira Valley. Even today there is a constant threat of rockfall, and the pass is regularly closed by snow in winter. But the completion of a viaduct from the Pass to the Otira River has eased the journey somewhat, and there are continued upgrades planned on the highway's difficult sections.

The most noticeable feature of this drive is the changing landscape as you progress westwards. Beyond the Canterbury Plains the highway climbs to open tussock grasslands beyond Porters Pass, and enters beech forest and high alpine terrain as it nears Arthur's Pass National Park. After the gradual rise through Canterbury's dry high-country landscape, the abrupt plunge toward the West Coast brings a rapid transition to dense rata and podocarp forests on this wetter side of the Alps.

Darfield
Try Darfield's Topiary Café for good food and coffee.

Springfield and the Canterbury Plains
Springfield (72 km from Christchurch) is the last town before the road climbs to Porters Pass. Springfield's tradition of hospitality dates to when horse-drawn Cobb & Co coaches travelled to and from the West Coast between 1866 and the 1920s. In keeping with this tradition, Springfield's Te Kowai Café serves up home-cooked food.

Porters Pass (945 m) – walks, picnicking
Beyond Springfield the highway approaches the Torlesse Range which features the distinctive square-cut Torlesse Gap – according to local legend flying through the gap has exercised a few daredevil pilots. The range is within the Torlesse Conservation Park, which protects the area's unique and rare alpine flora and fauna. SH 73 reaches Porters Pass and nearby Lake Lyndon at the southern end of the Torlesse range after a short haul from the plains. In winter this is a popular tobogganing and ski touring spot.

Kura Tawhiti Conservation Area – picnicking, walks
From Porters Pass the road sweeps towards Arthur's Pass along wide glaciated valleys. A few minutes drive from Porters is the turnoff to Porter Heights skifield, and shortly after on the left is Kura Tawhiti Conservation Area – a weird landscape of limestone boulders favoured by rock climbers, botanists and walkers. It is also a place revered by the West Coast's Waitaha tribe. Castle Hill village has no facilities for travellers.

Cave Stream – walks, picnicking
Limestone boulder fields, scarps and vast unbroken scree fields dominate the vistas over the next few kilometres between Castle Hill, Flock Hill and Craigieburn Forest Park. At Cave Stream Scenic Reserve,

up the hill from the Mt Cheeseman skifield turnoff, is a 'free caving' experience where in low flows it's possible to scramble through a limestone cave. Take a torch, wear strong shoes, dress for the wet and cold and don't attempt it when the river is high, if it's raining or looking like rain.

Craigieburn Forest Park/Flock Hill – campground, walks, skiing

Beech forests arrive on the landscape at Craigieburn Forest Park where an unserviced camping area is located a few minutes from Cave Stream. Access roads lead to Broken River and Craigieburn skifields, then after a short winding section is Flock Hill Station.

Flock Hill–Bealey – walks

Lake Pearson, home to a rare colony of crested grebe, is squeezed between hillsides and the long shifting screes on Purple Hill. Beyond here the route opens into space again toward Cass and the Waimakariri River. As the road edges past bluffs above the Waimakariri, horizons expand toward the Main Divide peaks, forests and tussock grasslands of Arthur's Pass. Just over Bruce Creek is a collection of holiday baches on Bealey Spur about a kilometre from the Bealey Hotel, where you can ask Paddy to tell you the one about the moa.

Arthur's Pass – walks, skiing

The highway enters the park at the Bealey Bridge over the Waimakariri. Klondyke Corner, the prominent forested corner on the opposite bank, has a camping ground and picnic area. Arthur's Pass village is located in the forested Bealey Valley 160 km from Christchurch. The park headquarters has information and excellent displays on the park's natural and human history. A Cobb & Co coach takes pride of place at the centre, which is a short distance from the railway tunnel (completed in 1923) that ended the era of horse-drawn transport over the pass. Of the short walks near the village, I would recommend the Devils Punchbowl Track (1.5 hours return). Oscar's Haus, named after local identity and prominent mountaineer, the late Oscar Coberger, is the pick of the village's cafés.

The Devils Punchbowl Falls

From the village SH 73 enters the alpine zone as it winds up the Pass (920 m). There is a superb lookout up the Bealey Valley. Although Maori have been using the pass for centuries, the memorial near the highpoint is to the explorer Arthur Dudley Dobson who was the first European to cross it, in 1864. The view of Mt Rolleston from the steep Temple Basin skifield track (3 hours return) is one of the best in the park. A more sedate but rewarding short walk can be enjoyed in the Upper Otira Valley which is peppered with alpine flowers in summer. NB: This is an alpine region and walkers should be equipped for mountain weather.

Otira Gorge

The descent into the Otira rapidly brings you to a vastly different milieu of huge boulders, rainforest and a dark, foreboding valley which is leavened in summer by bright displays of rata. The painter Petrus van der Velden's bleak representations of the valley in the 1890s (one of which is hung at Christchurch's Robert McDougall Art Gallery) will seem familiar when you've been here in a storm. Below the gorge, Otira settlement is an untidy collection of railways-related buildings and a pub.

Upper Otira Valley

From Otira, the highway turns west at Aickens where the Otira River meets the wide and braided Taramakau. Like Springfield, Jacksons Hotel 18 km from Otira, has long been a travellers' rest. From Jacksons, Greymouth is 62 km away via Kumara Junction and SH 6, or about 75 km via Moana and Lake Brunner.

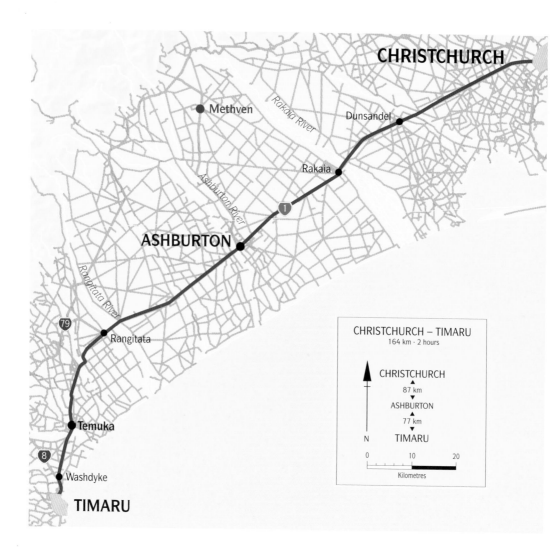

CHRISTCHURCH – TIMARU
164 km · 2 hours

N

CHRISTCHURCH
▲
87 km
▼
ASHBURTON
▲
77 km
▼
TIMARU

0   10   20
Kilometres

Christchurch–Dunedin SH 1
363 km, 5 hours

The drive south across the Canterbury Plains to Timaru is a necessary chore that must be endured to reach routes to Mount Cook, the Waitaki Valley, Central Otago, Dunedin and further south to the Catlins. Fortunately there are plenty of roadside fruit stalls and dairies for ice cream stops, as well as a choice of good cafés and good beaches to stop at south of Timaru. Most centres have playgrounds if the kids need to burn off some energy.

Christchurch–Timaru
164 km, 2 hours

Dunsandel
The Dunsandel Store has been converted into a fine travellers' café/delicatessen with good food, coffee, ice creams, juices and a pleasant courtyard out back.

Ashburton
Ashburton is about 1 hour from Christchurch. Turn off at Ashburton along SH 77 to reach Methven and Mt Hutt skifield. Ashburton's Botanic Gardens are well worth a visit. For a bite to eat try the Ashford Craft Village café on the bypass around the town, Kelly's Café and Bar on the main street or the Café Time Bakery just beyond the town centre in Tinwald.

Timaru
Those intending to drive to Mount Cook can take SH 79 between Rangitata, Geraldine and Fairlie (see Woodend–Geraldine, Route 47). Alternatively, you can take the longer route along SH 8 from Washdyke, shortly before Timaru (just over 2 hours from Christchurch). Timaru's Aigantighe Art Gallery is one of the country's best regional galleries. And look out for a bright yellow façade heralding Radiant Records on the outskirts of the city centre where you'll find a café and a superlative collection of CDs to choose from.

Timaru–Dunedin
South of Timaru, SH 1 follows coastal plains to the Waitaki River and Oamaru. There is an excellent walkway at Otaio Beach near Otaio settlement. Just before Hook is the Berry Barn Café, where you can also buy a range of seasonal berries. Thirty minutes from Timaru, just beyond Hook, SH 82 turns to Waimate township and up the north bank of the Waitaki River to Kurow (71 km from SH 1, see Omarama–Oamaru, Route 50).

Oamaru – campground, walks
Oamaru (3 hours from Christchurch) is world-renowned for its well-preserved collection of classical Victorian buildings made of 'Oamaru stone' (also called whitestone, a chalky limestone quarried in the district). The fully restored Harbour Street historic precinct houses several galleries, a pub and other shops – well worth a visit. Oamaru is the childhood home of the novelist Janet Frame and setting for many of her early novels – a heritage trail allows walkers to visit sites that feature in those works. This and other trails, including the 'Ocean to Alps' trail up the Waitaki Valley, are covered by the Heritage

Whitestone building, Oamaru

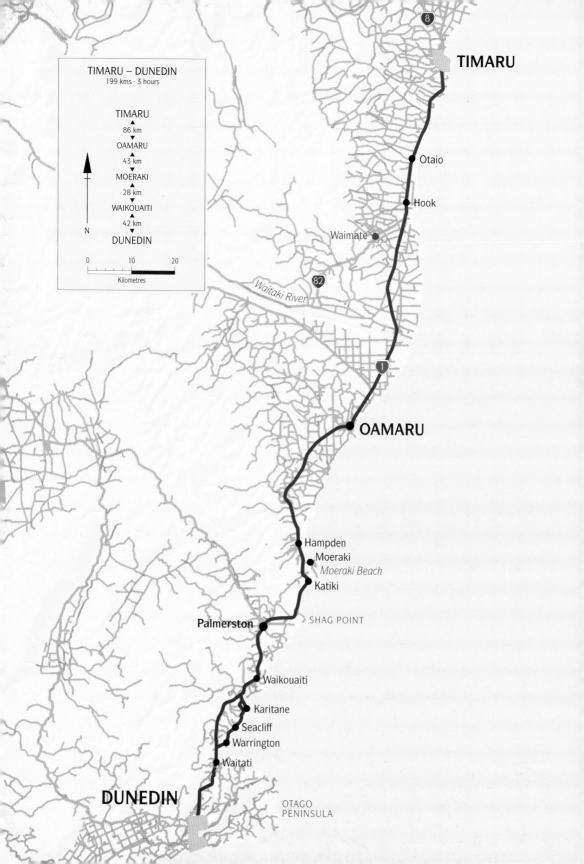

TIMARU – DUNEDIN
199 kms - 3 hours

TIMARU
▲
86 km
▼
OAMARU
▲
43 km
▼
MOERAKI
▲
28 km
▼
WAIKOUAITI
▲
42 km
▼
DUNEDIN

N

0   10   20
Kilometres

⑧

TIMARU

Otaio

Hook

Waimate

Waitaki River

㉒

①

OAMARU

Hampden

Moeraki

Moeraki Beach

Katiki

SHAG POINT

Palmerston

Waikouaiti

Karitane

Seacliff

Warrington

Waitati

DUNEDIN

OTAGO
PENINSULA

Trails of North Otago booklet (free at information centres). The opportunity to view blue and yellow-eyed penguins returning to their nests at dusk is another outstanding Oamaru attraction. For a bite to eat try the Delish Café opposite the railway station (corner of Ribble and Humber Streets).

Moeraki Boulders/Moeraki Village – campground, walks

The remarkable 60-million-year-old Moeraki Boulders are located on Moeraki Beach 43 km south of Oamaru, between Hampden and Moeraki village. The short walk along the beach to the boulders begins from a Department of Conservation carpark signposted off the highway (go straight ahead once you've turned off the highway). There is quicker access from the nearby café, but unless you are a café patron a donation is sought to cross land to reach the beach. The café is a missed opportunity – save your discretionary café dollars for Fleur's Place at Moeraki Village. The 45-minute Millenium Walkway offers a good introduction to the area – once the location of a large Maori settlement.

Moeraki boulders

Shag Point – walks, picnicking, wildlife

The association with Maori along this coast is continued as you drive south over a headland to the beautiful Katiki Beach and Shag Point, once a stronghold of a Ngai Tahu hapu or sub-grouping. The reef off the mouth of the Shag River is said to be the upturned hull of the Arai-te-Uru canoe, one of the great mythical waka that bore Maori's Polynesian ancestors to Aotearoa. A seal colony, sea lions and penguins can be observed from the Shag Point Scenic Reserve on the signposted side road around Shag Point towards the river mouth.

Palmerston & Waikouaiti

A short distance from Shag Point is the village of Palmerston (about 45 minutes before Dunedin). SH 85 – known to locals as 'the Pigroot' (apparently a reference to the number of pigs in the area in settler days) – leads westwards towards Ranfurly (see Route 55). Continuing south to Dunedin, SH 1 traverses hill country to Waikouaiti (Beanos Bakery is great, as is Waikouaiti Beach), returning to the coast at Waitati (Blueskin Bay), before climbing over Kilmog Hill to Dunedin.

Karitane–Warrington coast route – swimming, views

A short but scenic diversion south of Waikouaiti is the coastal drive from Karitane to Warrington. Karitane is a popular beach resort and fishing settlement with a long and interesting history. It was first colonised by Maori and later by whalers, then the South Island's first mission station was established here as settlers established themselves in the nineteenth century. Given this history the small museum at Seacliff is an interesting place to visit.

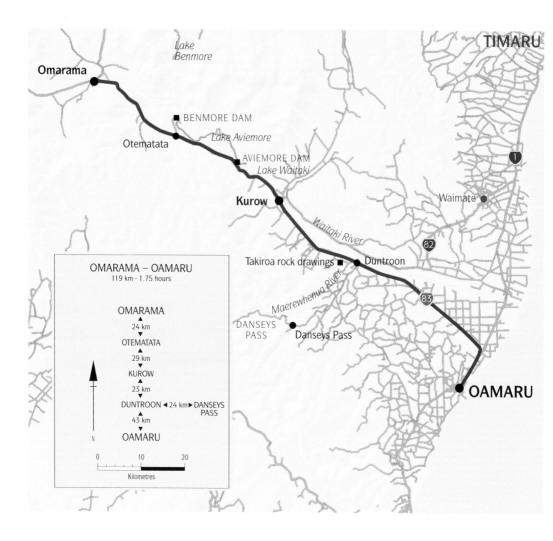

Lake
Benmore

TIMARU

Omarama

■ BENMORE DAM

Otematata

Lake Aviemore

AVIEMORE DAM
Lake Waitaki

Waimate ●

Kurow ●

Waitaki River

82

Takiroa rock drawings ■ ● **Duntroon**

Maerewhenua River

83

DANSEYS
PASS ● Danseys Pass

● **OAMARU**

OMARAMA – OAMARU
119 km - 1.75 hours

OMARAMA
▲
24 km
▼
OTEMATATA
▲
29 km
▼
KUROW
▲
23 km
▼
DUNTROON ◄ 24 km ► **DANSEYS
PASS**
▲
43 km
▼
OAMARU

N

0   10   20
Kilometres

Omarama–Oamaru SH 83
119 km, 1.75 hours

The drive down the Waitaki Valley from Omarama is flanked by stark high-country scenery and merino runs, but it's the artificial lakes of the Waitaki hydro scheme that dominate the landscape. The scheme produces one-third of New Zealand's electricity from eight power stations. Three hydro lakes – Benmore, Aviemore and Waitaki are on this route – (the remaining five power stations are in the upper Waitaki). The drive is covered by the 'Ocean to the Alps' heritage trail in the *Heritage Trails of North Otago* booklet (free from information centres).

Otematata/Benmore dam – swimming, fishing, boating

The first lake on the Waitaki is Lake Benmore, the largest of the country's hydro storage lakes, which is retained by one of the largest earth dams in the Southern Hemisphere (built in 1966). To reach Benmore dam turn off at Otematata. A visitor centre at the dam site makes good use of displays to describe the workings of the Waitaki scheme and electricity generation system to the North Island, but suffers from overzealous spin-doctoring about its environmental virtues. From here you can drive across the dam and around the northern shores of Lake Aviemore, returning to SH 83 at Aviemore. A short distance past Otematata is the fine Coffee Workshop Café (attached to the Challenge petrol station), which offers the best coffee in the Upper Waitaki, light meals, great cakes and other goodies.

Aviemore and Waitaki dams

The Aviemore dam, 19 km from Otematata, is an earth and concrete structure completed in 1969. Lake Waitaki, smallest of the three hydro lakes, filled the valley after the Waitaki dam was finished in 1934.

Kurow – campground

Kurow, with a population of about 411, is the largest centre in the valley. Many of its older buildings are constructed from Oamaru stone (see Oamaru above). From here the Waitaki River flows undammed to the sea: the trout and salmon fishing on the river is reputedly world class.

Takiroa Maori Rock Drawings

These well preserved charcoal and ochre rock drawings are found under a limestone overhang off the highway 3 km from Duntroon. While some drawings were unceremoniously chopped out of the wall and spirited to museums or private collections, the bulk remain. Interpretive panels describe the drawings and their origins.

Duntroon/Lower Waitaki – campground

Nicol's Blacksmith Shop with its working 19th-century forge, the Vanished World Museum and Flying Pig Café are worth setting aside time for a stop in Duntroon. Also worth considering is the scenic drive over Danseys Pass to Naseby and Ranfurly (SH 85, see also Dunedin–Cromwell via Middlemarch, Route 55). The route initially follows the Maerewhenua River to the Danseys Pass Holiday Park. Beyond here the road is unsealed and windy and should be driven carefully, if only to allow an appreciation of the wonderful tussock landscapes and schist

Danseys Pass (photo Dave Chowdhury)

outcrops on the pass. Not suitable for campervans. Allow 1.5 hours to Naseby.

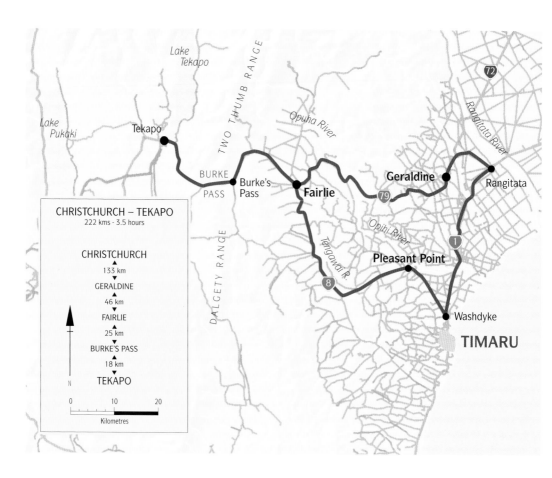

CHRISTCHURCH – TEKAPO
222 kms - 3.5 hours

CHRISTCHURCH
▲
133 km
▼
GERALDINE
▲
46 km
▼
FAIRLIE
▲
25 km
▼
BURKE'S PASS
▲
18 km
▼
TEKAPO

N

0   10   20
Kilometres

Christchurch–Wanaka SH 1, 79, 8
418 km, 6.5 hours

After climbing to the Mackenzie Basin from the Canterbury Plains, this drive traverses picturesque high country flanking the Southern Alps, past Aoraki/Mount Cook National Park and over Lindis Pass to Wanaka, base for excursions into Mount Aspiring National Park. The parks, mountain ranges and sequence of large glacial lakes are all part of the Te Wahipounamu South-West New Zealand World Heritage Area.

Christchurch–Tekapo, 222 km, 3.5 hours
From Christchurch take SH 1 south through Rakaia and Ashburton (see also Christchurch–Dunedin, Route 49). There are two routes to Fairlie from here. The first and quicker option is to leave SH 1 south of Rangitata and follow SH 79 to Fairlie via Geraldine (see Woodend–Geraldine, Route 47 for notes on Geraldine); the second is to continue to Washdyke and take SH 8.

From Geraldine the route to Fairlie leaves the flatlands and wends its way through farmed hill country to reach a high point overlooking the Opuha Valley (location of the Farm Barn Café) and the Two Thumb Range.

If driving from Washdyke, SH 8 to Fairlie allows easy travel up the Opihi and Tengawai valleys to Pleasant Point where the Pleasant Point steam railway operates in summer. The railway museum (at the station) doubles as an information centre. Pleasant Point's Old Post Office Coffee Shop behind the station is recommended.

Fairlie – campground

Marketed as the 'gateway' to the Mackenzie Country, Fairlie's greatest redeeming feature for travellers is the Old Library Café. Mackenzie was reputedly a wily Scottish drover cum sheep rustler whose legendary exploits led to his name being permanently fixed to the area.

Burke Pass and the Mackenzie Basin

The actual gateway to the Mackenzie Country is 25 km west of Fairlie at Burke Pass where SH 8 slips between the Two Thumb and Dalgety ranges. Below the pass on the Fairlie side is Burke's Pass settlement (tearooms). A description of the pass as a 'portal' is very apt, for here SH 8 enters the vast glaciated Mackenzie Basin, a region of lakes and undulating high-country grasslands below the Southern Alps. Shortly beyond the pass is a lookout offering a first view of Aoraki/Mt Cook.

Lake Tekapo – campground, fishing

Tekapo is a holiday destination where scenic flights and the stone Church of the Good Shepherd on the lakeshore are especially popular with tourists. Lake Tekapo is the first of three large glacial lakes in the basin, all of which have been harnessed by the Waitaki power scheme (see notes on Omarama–Oamaru, Route 50). Canals traverse the basin linking lakes with power stations, and long lines of pylons take the energy generated away.

Tekapo–Wanaka, 196 km, 3 hours

The 47 km drive from Tekapo across the Mackenzie Basin past Lake Pukaki to the turnoff to Aoraki/Mount Cook National Park takes 30–40 minutes. Chances are though you'll stop often to appreciate the expansive and arresting lake/grasslands/mountain vistas, even when clouds are pouring over the ranges during a nor'wester. An alternative route to Lake Pukaki (with great views of Aoraki/Mt Cook) is to drive along the Tekapo Canal to the Tekapo B power station on the eastern shore of Lake Pukaki – the canal drive (signposted 'Salmon Farm') begins about 13 km from Tekapo.

Aoraki/Mount Cook National Park – walks

Mount Cook Village is a 55 km (40-minute) drive along the western side of Lake Pukaki and the Tasman Valley. On a fine day this route offers stunning views of the national park's high peaks and glaciers including the country's highest mountain, Aoraki/Mt Cook (3755 m). Lake Pukaki fills the trench that formed when the Tasman Glacier retreated 10,000–13,000 years ago. The lake's level was artificially raised when the outlet was dammed for hydro-generation.

Aoraki/Mount Cook National Park is primarily an alpine climbing area, but there are a number of easy walks for the day visitor. Many of these, like the walks to Sealy Tarns or Blue Lakes on the Tasman Glacier, lead to interesting glacial landforms and fine views. Red Tarns, a steep 40 minute to 1 hour climb (one way), is well worth the effort for outstanding views of Aoraki/Mt Cook and Mt Sefton. Information about the park is available at the park visitor centre. Near the centre is The Old Mountaineers' Café. Rental car

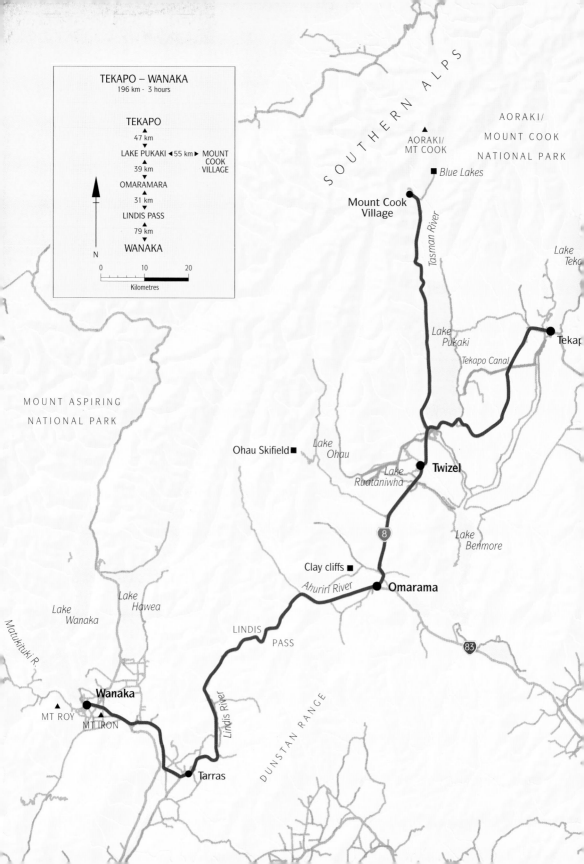

TEKAPO – WANAKA
196 km - 3 hours

TEKAPO
▲
47 km
▼
LAKE PUKAKI ◄ 55 km ► MOUNT
COOK
VILLAGE
39 km
▼
OMARAMARA
▲
31 km
▼
LINDIS PASS
▲
79 km
▼
WANAKA

N

0   10   20
Kilometres

SOUTHERN ALPS

AORAKI/
MOUNT COOK
NATIONAL PARK

AORAKI/
MT COOK ▲

■ Blue Lakes

Mount Cook
Village ●

Tasman River

Lake
Pukaki

Lake Teka

Tekapo Canal

Tekap ●

MOUNT ASPIRING

NATIONAL PARK

Ohau Skifield ■

Lake
Ohau

Lake
Ruataniwha

Twizel ●

8

Lake
Benmore

Clay cliffs ■

Ahuriri River

Omarama ●

83

Lake
Hawea

Lake
Wanaka

LINDIS

PASS

Lindis River

DUNSTAN RANGE

Matukituki R.

Wanaka ●

MT ROY ▲   ▲ MT IRON

Tarras ●

drivers should note that the Tasman Valley Road to the Tasman Glacier may be excluded from insurance cover – that said, the road is a straightforward drive as far as the Blue Lakes carpark.

Twizel – fishing

Twizel arose from the plains as a workers' village while the Waitaki power scheme was being constructed. It survives thanks to a steady tourism trade, the winter skiing industry based at the Ohau skifield, and New Zealanders who turned places vacated by redundant hydro workers into weekend holiday homes. Twizel is the base for a recovery programme for the critically endangered black stilt, a wading bird once common throughout New Zealand but now restricted to the braided rivers of the Mackenzie Basin. Guided tours of a captive rearing facility and viewing hide can be arranged from the Twizel Information Centre.

Lake Ohau & Clay Cliffs Reserve – walks, picnicking, fishing

From Twizel SH 8 continues south past Lake Ruataniwha. A side road 13 km from Twizel leads to the shores of Lake Ohau and to the Ohau skifield. Just before the Ahuriri River, prime black stilt habitat, signs indicate the way to the clay cliffs which are located on a side road above the Ahuriri River. Though on private land, this spectacular example of badland topography – deeply dissected ravines, pinnacles, gullies and sharp ridges eroded from gravels and silt – is protected by covenant, and is open to the public most of the year. Human connections with the cliffs area date to the earliest Polynesians who hunted moa and other birds from camps in the Waitaki Valley. Maori call the area Paritea, meaning white or light coloured cliff. A walking track leads into the heart of the cliffs area.

Omarama – fishing

Omarama has several tearooms, but the Clay Cliffs Estate Vineyard Café (500 m past Omarama, open from 11 a.m., closed Tuesdays and in winter) offers pleasant outdoor/indoor eating. Turn east from Omarama to reach SH 1 via the Waitaki Valley (SH 83, see Omarama–Oamaru, Route 50).

Lindis Pass (971 m)

The transition from the Canterbury high country into Central Otago's tawny tussock landscapes is made when SH 8 crosses Lindis Pass on the Dunstan Range. Much of the route over the pass occurs within Lindis Pass Scenic Reserve, which protects a large area of red-tussock grasslands. Over Lindis Pass SH 8 descends beside the Lindis River, a tributary of the Clutha. To reach Wanaka turn west on SH 8a just after Tarras (Country Coffee Shop, petrol, toilets).

Wanaka – campground, walks, fishing, skiing, boating

Wanaka is a sublime tourist town on the edge of Lake Wanaka, fourth largest lake in New Zealand. Drives around its southern shore and up the Matukituki Valley lead to Mount Aspiring National Park with fine views of Mt Aspiring. Walks in the Matukituki Valley, and (closer to Wanaka) to lookouts on Mt Roy (6 hours) and Mt Iron (45 minutes) offer spectacular views of the glaciated mountain scenery in this region. Of Wanaka's cafés, Kai Whaka Pai, on the lakefront, and the Green Room are the choice of discerning locals.

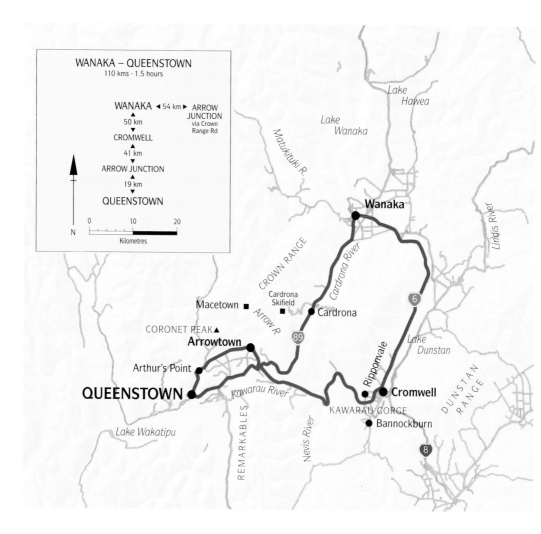

WANAKA – QUEENSTOWN
110 kms - 1.5 hours

WANAKA ◄ 54 km ► ARROW
▲   JUNCTION
50 km   via Crown
▼   Range Rd
CROMWELL
▲
41 km
▼
ARROW JUNCTION
▲
19 km
▼
QUEENSTOWN

N   0   10   20
     Kilometres

Wanaka–Queenstown

Both routes between these centres have their charms. The SH 6 route takes the traveller through wine and apricot-growing areas around Cromwell, and then through the Kawarau Gorge past historic mining sites and rugged Central Otago scenery. The Crown Range road (SH 89) is a scenic alpine route, which reaches the greatest elevation of any public road in New Zealand.

Wanaka–Queenstown SH 6
110 km, 1.5 hours

From Wanaka drive to Cromwell (50 km) along the shores of Lake Dunstan. Close to Cromwell are the Bannockburn and Ripponvale wine-growing areas. Bannockburn's Carrick and Mt Difficulty wineries have good cafés, while in Cromwell try the Fusee Rouge Café.

Kawarau Gorge

12 km from Cromwell at the entrance to the Kawarau Gorge is the Goldfields Mining Centre, a working gold claim where visitors can pan for gold, view mining relics and machinery. Keeping high on its left bank, SH 6 follows the Kawarau River as it flows through the gorge's narrow defile below steep and overhanging walls of layered schist. Beyond the Nevis River confluence the route crosses the Kawarau and follows open terraces where several well-known Central Otago vineyards – including Gibbston Valley and Chard Farm – are located. Where the gorge narrows again is the famous A.J. Hackett bungy jumping operation off the historic Victoria Bridge. The Crown Range route from Wanaka meets SH 6 at Arrow Junction near Arrowtown.

Arrowtown – campground, walks, picnicking, swimming

Arrowtown is a picturesque holiday village, a short distance from SH 6, and 19 km from Queenstown. The area's colourful goldmining past is recreated at the town's museum, while walks towards Macetown reveal mining relics. There's pleasant swimming and picnicking by the Arrow River.

Crown Range Road SH 89
54 km (to SH 6 at Arrowtown), 1 hour

This scenic traverse of the Crown Range offers a quick route to Queenstown. It travels south from Wanaka up the Cardrona Valley, past the historic Cardrona Hotel and the Cardrona Skifield. The climb through tussock landscapes to the crest of the Crown Range reaches 1121 m with spectacular views over Lake Wakatipu, The Remarkables and the area's glacial landforms. The descent toward Arrowtown is steep, culminating in a zigzag below Crown Terrace to SH 6.

Queenstown

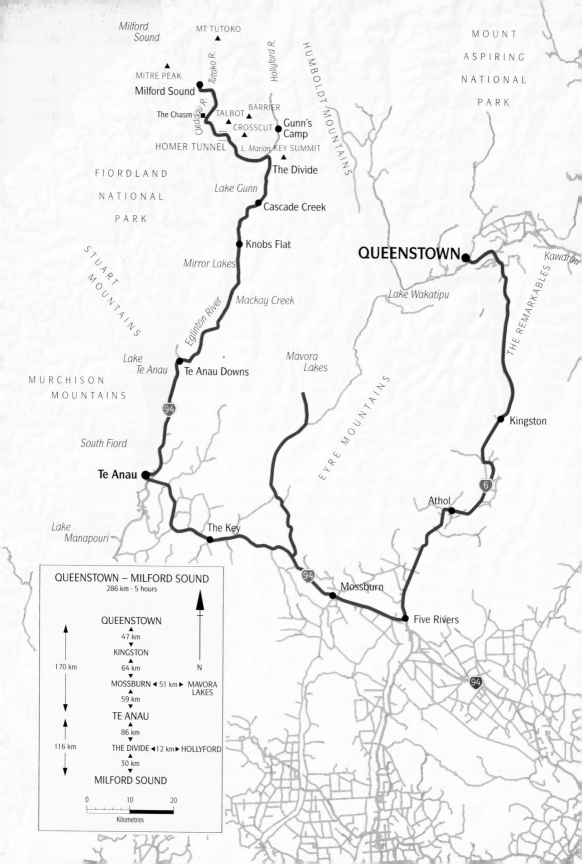

Milford Sound

MT TUTOKO

MITRE PEAK

Milford Sound

The Chasm   TALBOT   BARRIER   Gunn's Camp
CROSSCUT

HOMER TUNNEL   L. Marian   KEY SUMMIT

The Divide

Lake Gunn

Cascade Creek

Knobs Flat

Mirror Lakes

Mackay Creek

Te Anau Downs

Lake
Te Anau

94

South Fiord

Te Anau

Lake
Manapouri

The Key

FIORDLAND

NATIONAL

PARK

STUART

MOUNTAINS

MURCHISON
MOUNTAINS

Tutoko R.

Cleddau R.

Hollyford R.

Eglinton River

HUMBOLDT MOUNTAINS

MOUNT

ASPIRING

NATIONAL

PARK

QUEENSTOWN

Lake Wakatipu

Kawarau

THE REMARKABLES

Kingston

6

Athol

EYRE MOUNTAINS

Mavora
Lakes

Mossburn

Five Rivers

94

94

QUEENSTOWN – MILFORD SOUND

286 km · 5 hours

QUEENSTOWN
▲
47 km
▼
KINGSTON
▲
64 km
▼
MOSSBURN ◄ 51 km ► MAVORA
LAKES
▲
59 km
▼
TE ANAU
▲
86 km
▼
THE DIVIDE ◄ 12 km ► HOLLYFORD
▲
30 km
▼
MILFORD SOUND

170 km

116 km

N

0   10   20

Kilometres

Queenstown–Milford Sound SH 6, 94
286 km, 5 hours

The 116 km Te Anau–Milford Highway in Fiordland National Park is undoubtedly one of the most rewarding drives in New Zealand. When it's fine the route combines spectacular mountain and forest scenery with some very good short walks and camping areas. In the wet, mountainsides become laced with waterfalls, and while driving may require more care, it is never dull. Fiordland incorporates almost half the 2.6 million ha Te Wahipounamu South-West New Zealand World Heritage Area, which recognises the outstanding natural and cultural features of this extraordinary landscape. For most tourists, Milford Sound is the 'must-visit' scenic icon of New Zealand, and because of that you must also put up with the worst aspects of mass tourism – crowds, tour buses, and noisy aircraft.

Queenstown–Te Anau (3 hours)
To reach Te Anau from Queenstown take SH 6 along the southern arm of Lake Wakatipu, past Kingston to Five Rivers. Here you turn off to Mossburn where SH 94 leads across undulating farmland beneath the Takitimu Mountains to Te Anau. The drive around Lake Wakatipu is the most scenic part of this leg, with its views to the Eyre Mountains.

Kingston
There are several lake-edge picnic sites near and at Kingston, home of the Kingston Flyer, a vintage steam train service which puffs its way to Fairlight and back in 90 minutes. Departs daily at 10 a.m., 1.30 p.m. and 3.45 p.m. There's a tavern and café at the Kingston Station.

Athol
Were it not for the Lazybones Café, Athol, just under an hour from Queenstown, would be of little interest to travellers. But this is an excellent roadside eatery, and if leaving Queenstown early I'd recommend skipping that expensive Queenstown breakfast and heading straight to Athol to experience fine country cooking and mastery of the espresso machine.

Mavora Lakes – campground, walks, picnicking
The Mavora Lakes Park is 39 km along an easy unsealed road that leaves SH 94 about 12 km from Mossburn. It is a wonderful location, beech forested, and great for swimming, picnicking and fishing.

Beyond the Mavora Lakes' turnoff, SH 94 passes briefly through the Red Tussock Conservation Area, and from near The Key come first views of the Fiordland mountains.

Te Anau – campground, walks, picnicking
On the south-eastern shores of Lake Te Anau, this township is a very busy tourist centre in the summer months. The Fiordland National Park visitor centre is located near the eastern outskirts of the town, close to the DoC-run Te Anau Wildlife Centre where a number of native bird species can be viewed in aviaries. Among them are takahe, a critically endangered species whose only wild population is across Lake Te Anau in the Murchison Mountains. The Olive Tree Café on the main street has been a consistently good

eatery over the years, while the newer Naturally Fiordland café offers great cakes, juices, smoothies and coffee you can taste.

Milford Highway

If you're not rushing to catch a tour boat you can avoid choking on diesel fumes from the 90 or so tour buses that travel the highway daily (in summer), by leaving Te Anau around 2 p.m., when most are on the return journey. Without stopping you can reach Milford Sound in about 2 hours, but you'd be missing plenty. DoC has published a good brochure on the history, natural features, short walks, campsites and other aspects of the highway. The sandflies are savage – repellent is a must for walkers and campers. Buy fuel at Te Anau – the return journey is within the range of most vehicles though fuel can be purchased (at great cost) at Milford or Gunn's Camp. In winter, the road may be closed by avalanches or snow.

The first leg of the journey to Milford is alongside Lake Te Anau, with views early on across the lake up the South Fiord and to the Stuart and Murchison mountains. Milford Track walkers need drive no further than Te Anau Downs, 30 minutes from Te Anau. From here the highway shifts inland past recovering stands of forest to the darker red beech forests of the Eglinton Valley.

Mackay Creek – campsites, walks, views, picnicking

The open grassy expanses of the river flats at Mackay Creek offer the first significant view of Fiordland's dramatic landscapes, which like the rest of the Southern Alps were carved by vast glaciers. What's different is that the erosion-resistant qualities of Fiordland's granite, gneiss and diorite rocks have preserved the glacial imprint in its steep walls, summits and U-shaped valleys – when elsewhere in the South Island softer rocks have given way to a less angular topography.

Mirror Lakes – campsites, walks, views

A five-minute boardwalk excursion to a valley-edge wetland, with clear pools containing trout and waterfowl (including scaup, mallard and shags). Forest birds flit through red and silver beech forest, from common tomtits and fantails to the rare rifleman.

Knobs Flat – shelter, campsite

A public shelter here has panels describing the road's history, the work of avalanche controllers, natural history and the world heritage area.

Lake Gunn

The 45-minute Lake Gunn nature walk (76 km from Te Anau) is accessible to wheelchairs.

The Divide – shelter, walks

The Divide is the forest pass separating the Eglinton and Hollyford valleys. It is the start/finish point for the Routeburn and Greenstone tracks, as well as the popular walk to Key Summit (3 hours return), a sub-alpine wetland offering outstanding views of Fiordland and north towards Mount Aspiring National Park. From the Divide, SH 94 enters the most spectacular section of the highway, beginning with the steep descent to the Hollyford River. 'Pops View' is a well-situated lookout with vistas east to the Humboldt Mountains, and west towards the U-shaped hanging valley of Marian Creek below Mt Crosscut.

Hollyford Valley – campground, walks

The Hollyford Road (unsealed) branches off northwards at the base of the descent. A 10-minute forest walk along the Lake Marian track, about a kilometre from the junction, crosses the Hollyford to reach a spectacular cataract. Gunn's Camp, 8 km from the junction, features a campground, store, a great little museum, and the droll humour of camp-owner Mr Murray Gunn.

From the junction SH 94 climbs the steep fall of the Hollyford River to the subalpine grass and shrublands of the upper Hollyford Valley. Near the Homer Tunnel, the prominent pyramid of Mt Talbot overlooks boulder fields and vegetation decimated by winter and spring avalanches. On the right, up the Gertrude Valley, is the aptly named Mt Barrier.

Homer Tunnel & Cleddau Valley – walks

Homer Tunnel, constructed between 1934 and 1954, bores through Homer Saddle to the Cleddau Valley. At the carpark at the Hollyford end you'll quite likely encounter inquisitive kea, a mountain parrot, but please observe the entreaty not to feed them. At the tunnel's western end the road emerges into the breathtaking Cleddau Valley and starts a winding descent to the Cleddau River. In a storm the sight of waterfalls cascading thousands of metres down the bluffs is unforgettable.

The short walk to The Chasm takes you to where the Cleddau River is forced through a slot gorge. As you descend through forests toward Milford Sound there are occasional sightings of snowcapped Mt Tutoko (2746 m), the highest peak in Fiordland – best viewed from the Tutoko River bridge. Just past the Donne River are first views of Mitre Peak.

Milford Sound – campground, walks, boat tours

It's not possible for the overexposure of Mitre Peak and Milford Sound in countless brochures, posters and tourist department advertisements to take anything away from your first sight of them. Milford is busy and noisy, but if you can stay longer than an hour, you'll find a moment of quiet and perhaps some solitude on a walk to appreciate how wonderful the place is.

The best place for lunch or a meal is at Milford Sound 'Lodge', a backpacker hostel and campground located a kilometre back up the road.

Mitre Peak, Milford Sound

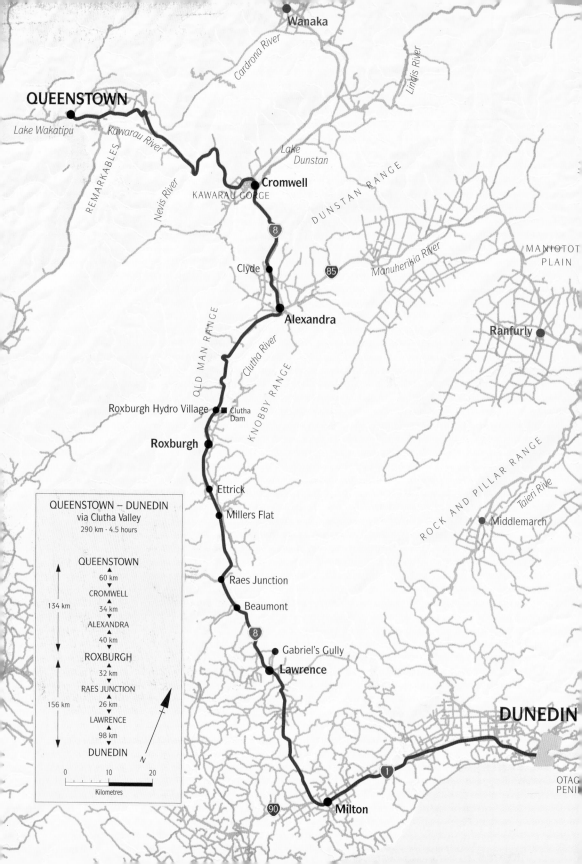

QUEENSTOWN
Wanaka
Cardrona River
Lindis River

Lake Wakatipu
Kawarau River
REMARKABLES
Nevis River
Lake Dunstan
Cromwell
KAWARAU GORGE
DUNSTAN RANGE
MANIOTOT PLAIN

8
Clyde
85
Manuherikia River
Ranfurly

Alexandra
OLD MAN RANGE
Clutha River
KNOBBY RANGE

Roxburgh Hydro Village
Clutha Dam
ROCK AND PILLAR RANGE
Taieri River

Roxburgh
Middlemarch

Ettrick

Millers Flat

Raes Junction

Beaumont
8
Gabriel's Gully
Lawrence
DUNEDIN

1
OTAG PENI

90
Milton

QUEENSTOWN – DUNEDIN
via Clutha Valley
290 km · 4.5 hours

QUEENSTOWN	
60 km	
CROMWELL	
34 km	134 km
ALEXANDRA	
40 km	
ROXBURGH	
32 km	
RAES JUNCTION	
26 km	156 km
LAWRENCE	
98 km	
DUNEDIN	

N

0   10   20
Kilometres

Queenstown–Dunedin via Clutha Valley SH 8
290 km, 4.5 hours

Queenstown to Alexandra (94 km) is a scenic 1.5 hour drive through the Kawarau Gorge to Cromwell and along the shores of Lake Dunstan (this leg of the route is described in the Wanaka–Queenstown, Route 52 and Cromwell–Dunedin, Route 55 sections).

From Alexandra, SH 8 travels south down the Clutha Valley, renowned for its orchards, brown trout and quinnat salmon fishing, and jet boating on the Clutha River. Between Alexandra and Roxburgh the route tracks through a distinctive Central Otago landscape, flanked on the west by the Old Man Range and on the east by the Knobby Range. There are expansive views over the Clutha, undulating grasslands and outcrops of schist. You can sample this landscape on the 40-minute interpreted walk at the Flat Top Hill Conservation Area 6 km from Alexandra. It's worth having the Clutha District Heritage Trail brochure on hand if you're interested in the area's gold mining past.

Roxburgh – campground

Lake Roxburgh was formed when the Clutha was dammed near Roxburgh in the early 1950s – at one stage this was the largest dam in New Zealand (the largest now is Benmore in the Waitaki Valley). Near the dam is the Jailhouse Café. Award-winning Succulents Café is located in Roxburgh township, 40 km from Alexandra, the centre of the valley's pipfruit growing industry. Tours of Roxburgh's orchards and gardens are a popular activity and there is a museum situated in a former Methodist Church (1872). The Lake Roxburgh walkway offers another opportunity to stretch your legs.

Roxburgh–Lawrence

SH 8 continues southwards through Ettrick and Millers Flat (dairy, campground, pub). At Raes Junction, 72 km from Alexandra, SH 90 turns off to Gore (67 km – gallery and café at Tapanui). A little further down the road, SH 8 crosses the Clutha at the historic Beaumont Bridge (1887). Next to the bridge is the start of the Millenium Track, which wanders down the Clutha's east bank.

Lawrence

Lawrence etched its place in New Zealand history when gold was struck in nearby Gabriel's Gully in May 1861 – a discovery that helped lift New Zealand out of economic depression and brought 10,000 diggers to the area. Gabriel's Gully is a short drive from Lawrence, with interpreted walking tracks and a great picnic spot. Lawrence has two good cafés, including Jazzed on Java. SH 1 is joined 37 km from Lawrence, just south of Milton, and 50 minutes (61 km) drive from Dunedin.

Schist outcrop, Central Otago

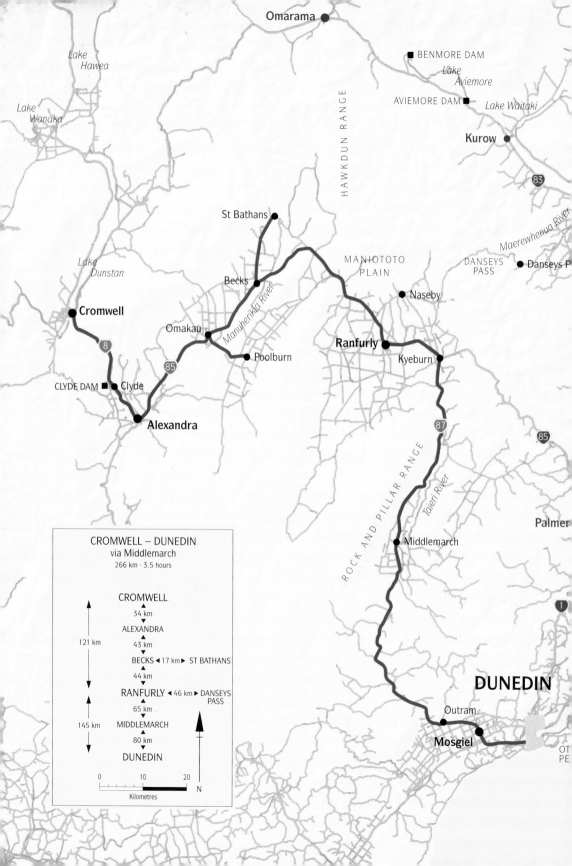

Lake Hawea

Lake Wanaka

Omarama

■ BENMORE DAM
Lake Aviemore
AVIEMORE DAM ■ *Lake Waitaki*

Kurow

83

HAWKDUN RANGE

Maerewhenua River

St Bathans

Lake Dunstan

Cromwell

8

Becks

Manuherikla River

Omakau

Poolburn

MANIOTOTO PLAIN

Naseby

DANSEYS PASS

Danseys P

Ranfurly

Kyeburn

85

CLYDE DAM ■ Clyde

85

Alexandra

87

ROCK AND PILLAR RANGE

Taieri River

Middlemarch

85

Palmer

1

DUNEDIN

Outram

Mosgiel

OT PE

CROMWELL – DUNEDIN
via Middlemarch
266 km · 3.5 hours

CROMWELL
▲
34 km
▼
ALEXANDRA
▲
121 km
43 km
▲
BECKS ◄17 km► ST BATHANS
▼
44 km
▼
RANFURLY ◄46 km► DANSEYS PASS
▲
65 km
145 km
MIDDLEMARCH
▲
80 km
▼
DUNEDIN

0   10   20
Kilometres
N

Cromwell–Dunedin via Middlemarch SH 8, 85, 87
266 km, 3.5 hours

This route traverses Central Otago where wide undulating valleys float between dun-coloured ranges — landscapes turned mythical by the Lord of the Rings films, painter Grahame Sydney and the makers of car and beer ads.

Clyde/Alexandra – campground

From Cromwell it's a 20-minute drive around Lake Dunstan to Clyde and Alexandra. Clyde has shaken its recent hydro-town past and reverted to sleepy holidaysville with several traveller's cafés (try the Post Office or the Clyde Courthouse cafés on Blyth Street), and old stone buildings made straight out of the schist landscape. All of which neatly complements nearby Alexandra's wine and historical trails and roadside stalls selling apricots and other stone fruits for which the area is famous.

Omakau

For fine views of the Central Otago landscape, turn right at Omakau and drive 4 km toward Poolburn to the crest of the Ragged Ridge.

St Bathans – walks, picnicking, swimming

SH 85 continues up the Manuherikia Valley alongside sheep-runs and localities with little more than a pub to their name. Historic St Bathans, 17 km off the highway (sealed) from Becks, is one of the best preserved sites in the Otago Goldfields Park. The town's collection of nineteenth-century wooden, stone and mudbrick buildings stands on the edge of disused goldworkings that date to the 1860s gold rush. The rustic mudbrick Vulcan Hotel (1882) and the Post Office (1909) are still open for business.

Ranfurly/Naseby – walks, biking, fishing, panning, campground

From Becks, SH 85 rounds Ragged Ridge and North Rough Ridge and enters the expansive tussock grass-lands of the Maniototo Plain beneath the Hawkdun Range. Ranfurly has reinvented itself as a centre for rural art deco, has an interesting railway station museum and the newish Central Café. Naseby, 14 km north of Ranfurly near the Naseby pine plantation, is a lovely village with period buildings, craft shops, a village green, the Cottage Garden Café (recommended) and the Royal Hotel. The historic Danseys Pass Hotel and Kyeburn Gold Diggings is 20 minutes from Naseby along a rough unsealed road. (Allow 45 minutes to reach Palmerston and SH 1 from Ranfurly.)

Middlemarch – walks

Just past Kyeburn turn south onto SH 87 for the 129 km/1.5 hour drive through Middlemarch to Mosgiel and Dunedin. Flanked by the Rock and Pillar Range, SH 87 follows the meandering Taieri River and the justly popular Central Otago Rail Trail — an old railway route developed into a walking track and mountain bike trail. Beyond Middlemarch (Kissing Gate Café) the highway climbs through rolling hills, offering fine views back towards the Maniototo before it descends to Outram and Mosgiel to join SH 1.

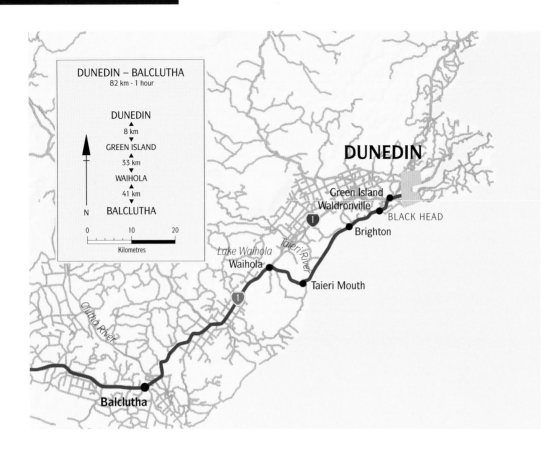

DUNEDIN – BALCLUTHA
82 km - 1 hour

DUNEDIN
▲
8 km
▼
GREEN ISLAND
▲
33 km
▼
WAIHOLA
▲
41 km
▼
BALCLUTHA

N

0   10   20

Kilometres

Dunedin–Invercargill SH 1
219 km, 3 hours

Dunedin–Taieri Mouth–Lake Waihola

The quickest route from Dunedin to Invercargill is by SH 1 across the Taieri Plains, but there's a worthwhile coastal variation that follows the 'Southern Scenic Route' along the coast south of Dunedin as far as Taieri Mouth. Look for the Southern Scenic Route turnoff from SH 1 south of the city centre and make for Waldronville. Black Head is an impressive basalt cliff east of Waldronville – well worth the few extra minutes required to divert there. The route passes the beach resort of Brighton (store) and follows the beautiful sandy coastline to Taieri Mouth. Here it turns inland to Lake Waihola (unsealed for 12 km, excellent views) where it rejoins SH 1. Walks up to 4 hours can be made in the Taieri River gorge. Camping and picnicking sites are located at Taieri Mouth and Brighton. Lake Waihola is a popular recreation area, and birdwatchers will enjoy a visit to the Sinclair Wetlands near here.

Balclutha – campground

From Balclutha (try The Gate café), SH 1 heads west toward Clinton and Gore through the rolling country landscape made prosperous by Southland's wool-growers. The stretch between Clinton and Gore was

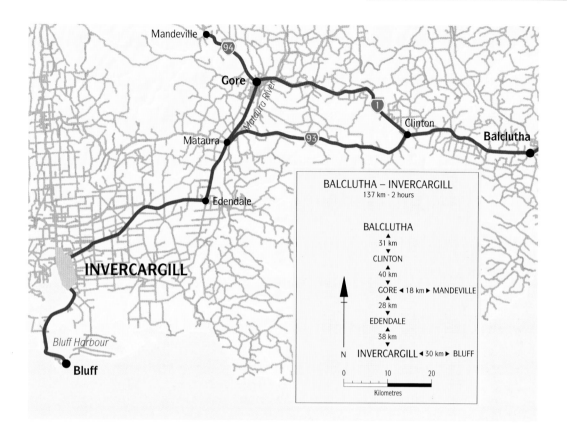

BALCLUTHA – INVERCARGILL
137 km - 2 hours

BALCLUTHA
▲
31 km
▼
CLINTON
▲
40 km
▼
GORE ◄ 18 km ► MANDEVILLE
▲
28 km
▼
EDENDALE
▲
38 km
▼
INVERCARGILL ◄ 30 km ► BLUFF

N

0   10   20
Kilometres

declared the 'Presidential Highway' when President Clinton visited New Zealand in 1999. From Clinton, SH 93 offers a bypass to Mataura (1 hour).

Gore – campground

Gore is a pleasant town on the banks of the Mataura River, a renowned brown trout fishery. The modern, well-designed Hokonui Moonshine Museum is a must-stop attraction that recounts Gore's colourful history as the centre of an illicit trade moonshining whisky during the area's 'dry' years. Over the road, Gore's innovative Eastern Southland Gallery houses New Zealand's only permanent collection of paintings by Ralph Hotere; it also has an extraordinary collection of paintings – including works by Rita Angus and Theo Schoon and indigenous art from African, Aboriginal and pre-Colombian societies – donated to the gallery by John Money. Ten minutes from Gore on SH 94, Croydon Air Services welcomes casual visitors to its vintage aircraft restoration workshop at Mandeville Airfield – Tiger Moths are a speciality, as are joyride flights. An aircraft museum is now being planned for the site. The adjacent café is a good one, and so is the Post Office café in town.

From Gore, Invercargill is about 40 minutes via Mataura and Edendale. Bluff, at the end of SH 1 is 20 minutes from Invercargill.

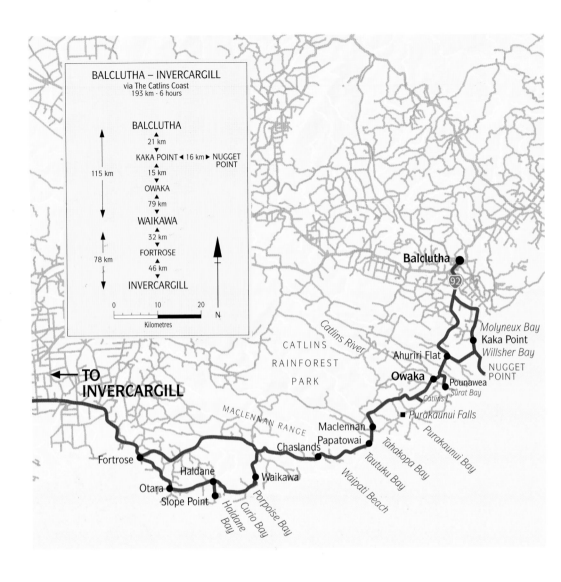

BALCLUTHA – INVERCARGILL
via The Catlins Coast
193 km - 6 hours

BALCLUTHA
▲ 21 km ▼
KAKA POINT ◄ 16 km ► NUGGET POINT
115 km
▲ 15 km ▼
OWAKA
▲ 79 km ▼
WAIKAWA
78 km
▲ 32 km ▼
FORTROSE
▲ 46 km ▼
INVERCARGILL

0   10   20
Kilometres   N

Balclutha–Invercargill via the Catlins Coast SH 92
193 km (approximately), 6 hours

The southeast corner of the South Island is a remarkably beautiful area renowned for its coastal forests, wildlife, beaches and scenery. Mercifully, the Catlins hasn't been subjected to excessive tourism development. What services exist for tourists – the campgrounds, backpackers, homestays and specialist 'eco-tourism' operations are small-scale and low impact, and this feels right for the area. Tourists and providers of small-scale accommodation cottoned on to the potential of the Catlins long before local tourism planners – so much so that the Southern

Scenic Route, the premiere touring route through the Catlins still has a lengthy section that is unsealed, as are most of the side routes to the coast and link roads. Even more bizarrely, the official route bypasses some of the Catlins' most scenic locations. This being the case it requires map-reading and careful driving on gravel roads to experience the best from a visit here.

Kaka Point/Nugget Point – campground, walks, views, swimming, patrolled beach

From Balclutha drive south on SH 92 and take the turnoff 6 km from Balclutha to Kaka Point village (15 km from turnoff) on the edge of Molyneux Bay where there is a pleasant beach, store, The Point Café and a kids' playground. From here it's an increasingly spectacular 16 km drive around the coast to Nugget Point. Nugget Point lighthouse, built in 1869, is an airy but quite safe five-minute walk from the carpark. Fur and elephant seals, New Zealand sea lions, and blue and yellow-eyed penguins are often resident here. Back toward Kaka Point a track leads to the Roaring Bay penguin viewing hides, best used at dusk when penguins are coming ashore.

Nugget Point

Owaka, Pounawea and Surat Bay – campground, walks, swimming

To reach Owaka from Kaka Point, take the gravel road from Willsher Bay to SH 92 at Ahuriri Flat. Cannibal Bay Beach (signposted) is a wild beach 8 km from the main road. Owaka (15 km from Kaka Point) is the largest settlement in the Catlins with most services tourists require.

To get to Pounawea, Jacks Blowhole and Surat Bay (on the shores of the Catlins River estuary) turn east at Owaka. There's a campground and safe swimming at Pounawea, while at Surat Bay near the Catlins Heads, New Zealand sea lions are often encountered lounging on the inner beach during summer (while rarely known to have a go at humans, it still pays to give them a wide berth). The beach walk from Surat Bay backpacker lodge to the outer coast is a highlight, particularly when the sea lions are about.

Purakaunui Falls/Purakaunui Bay – campground, walks, picnicking

Just past Catlins Lake (the head of the Catlins River estuary), leave SH 92 again and take the signposted road to Purakaunui Falls. The tarmac soon ends as the road winds toward the remnant beech forest containing the track to the falls (20 minutes return). Before the falls a road leads to Purakaunui Bay where there is a lovely beach with camping and picnicking areas. If you decide to bypass the falls, the main road to Tahakopa Bay crosses Gibbs Hill and the forested Table Hill Scenic reserve (look out for the Matai Falls short walk).

Tahakopa Bay/Papatowai – campground, walks, picnicking

From the Purakaunui Falls carpark, take the left fork and continue along the unsealed route to Maclennan on the edge of the Catlins Coastal Rainforest Park. At the bridge over the forest fringed estuary formed by the Tahakopa River is a carpark and the start of the 'Old Coach Road' walk. This is an easy forest walk (40 minutes return) to the river mouth and Tahakopa Bay beach, the site of an early Polynesian moa-hunter camp.

Over the bridge, Papatowai is a small holiday settlement with a pleasant beach-side picnicking spot beneath the totara trees at Picnic Point (kids playground nearby on Mirren Street), and opportunity for long beach walks. On Cross Street (up the hill from the beach access) is the 35-minute Picnic Point forest walk. Blair Somerville's Lost Gypsy Gallery never fails to entertain with his collection of curious creations, devices, gadgets and gizmos. Papatowai once supported a considerable Maori population in pre-European times — from the bones that have been unearthed here it's thought this was one of the last moa habitats in New Zealand.

Tautuku Bay – walks, swimming
The tarmac ends just beyond Papatowai and isn't regained until Chaslands. Be wary of truckies and others who travel this road at speed. From Papatowai there's a dusty 2 km climb up Florence Hill to the wonderful viewpoint overlooking Tautuku Beach, Tautuku Peninsula and forest from the coast to the Maclennan Range — welcome respite from the sparseness of the farmed landscape encountered on much of the drive thus far. The turnoff to Tautuku Beach is not far down the hill. As well as the beach there are two quality walks from the road worth considering: Lake Wilkie, a 20-minute forest walk; and the Tautuku estuary boardwalk (also 20 minutes).

Cathedral Caves – walk
Beyond Tautuku Bay, the road crosses a forested range in the Tautuku Scenic Reserve in which rimu, kamahi and roadside groves of fuchsia are striking features. 12 km from Papatowai is the access to Cathedral Caves at Waipati Beach. The access track crosses private land and is opened only when tides allow. There is a small charge ($3 in 2004) for crossing the land, well worth it for the 25-minute walk along a well-made track to these beautiful limestone caves. Ask at information centres for access details and tide details.

Waikawa/Curio Bay – campground, walks, swimming
The tarmac is regained soon after the road crosses Chaslands, a farmed area entirely surrounded by forest. The T-junction at the conclusion of the forest portion of this drive offers the choice of continuing west along the Southern Scenic Route to Invercargill (80 km), or the more interesting option of heading south to Waikawa, Curio Bay and the coastal route to Fortrose. Towards Waikawa, not far from the junction, is the Catlins' best eatery, the Niagara Falls Café and Gallery.

Waikawa, 6 km from the junction, has a small café/information centre and museum. Curio Bay, the settlement on the shores of Porpoise Bay, is famous for its surf beach, rare Hector's dolphins, yellow-eyed and blue penguins, seals and the nearby fossil forest.

Seeing the 20 or so Hector's dolphins resident in Porpoise Bay is a delight but there is increasing concern about the impact of tourism on them. Being inshore feeders they will often be seen in the surf — this is the only place in the country where dolphins venture so close in. Given the small size of the group here, and because the species overall is so perilously close to extinction, humans must make a special effort not to disturb these creatures. Indeed, guidebooks promoting the bay as a place to swim with dolphins have caused much alarm. DoC's guidelines stipulate that Hector's dolphins shouldn't be fed, touched or approached (they will move toward you if they want to). Lastly, don't enter the water within 50 m of a dolphin.

The 180-million-year-old fossilised forest exposed on the outgoing tide at Curio Bay is another of the area's internationally significant marvels. This is part of one of the largest and least-disturbed Jurassic-era fossil forests in the world – stumps, entire trunks and root systems can be discerned in the rock platform and cliffs. The story of the forest is recounted on the information panel at the bay. Unfortunately too many people are venturing into the nearby penguin area and disturbing the easily spooked birds as they come ashore in the evenings. Tourists are now being asked to not go down to the forest area after 5 p.m.

Slope Point – walk

From Curio Bay the travel is again on unsealed roads for approximately 15 km towards Otara. Below another large remnant of forest, the route skirts a dune lake and the tidal estuary inland of Haldane Bay, and eventually reaches a T-junction at Haldane. From here you can make a brief 5-km diversion toward Slope Point, the most southerly point of the South Island. Even if you don't make the 10-minute walk across farmland to the Point (closed in September and October) the drive offers fine views of the coast, Foveaux Strait and Stewart Island. The Southern Scenic Route is joined again at Fortrose, northwest of Otara and 46 km from Invercargill.

Tautuku Beach, Catlins (photo Dave Chowdhury)

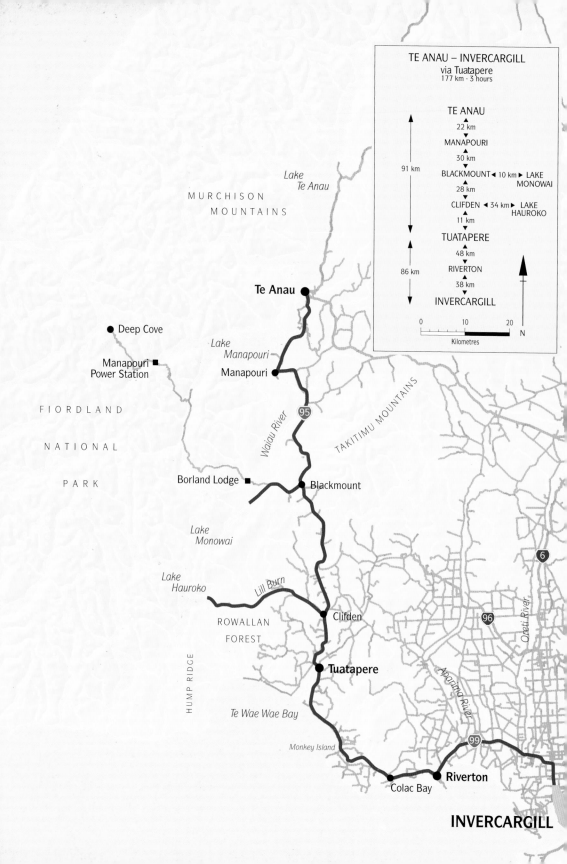

MURCHISON MOUNTAINS

Lake Te Anau

Te Anau

Deep Cove

Manapouri Power Station

Lake Manapouri

Manapouri

F I O R D L A N D

N A T I O N A L

P A R K

Waiau River

TAKITIMU MOUNTAINS

Borland Lodge

Blackmount

Lake Monowai

Lake Hauroko

Lill Burn

ROWALLAN

FOREST

Clifden

HUMP RIDGE

Tuatapere

Te Wae Wae Bay

Monkey Island

Aparima River

Oreti River

Colac Bay

Riverton

INVERCARGILL

TE ANAU – INVERCARGILL
via Tuatapere
177 km - 3 hours

TE ANAU
22 km
MANAPOURI
30 km
BLACKMOUNT ◄ 10 km ► LAKE MONOWAI
28 km
CLIFDEN ◄ 34 km ► LAKE HAUROKO
11 km
TUATAPERE
48 km
RIVERTON
38 km
INVERCARGILL

91 km

86 km

0   10   20
Kilometres

N

95

6

96

99

Te Anau–Invercargill via Tuatapere SH 95, 99
177 km, 3 hours

This route (the western leg of Southland's 'Southern Scenic Route') follows the forested eastern edge of Fiordland down the Waiau Valley to Te Wae Wae Bay. Scenic highlights are the beautiful glacier-formed lakes: Manapouri, Monowai and Hauroko.

Manapouri – campground, walks, swimming, fishing
Manapouri, 22 km from Te Anau on the edge of Lake Manapouri, is part tourist centre, hydro village and holiday home location. Although its lake, forest and mountain scenery is no less stunning than Te Anau, Manapouri has the virtue of being a far quieter place. Most come here to make the lake cruise to the Manapouri Power Station and the spectacular tour from the station to Deep Cove.

Lake Monowai – campground, picnicking, fishing
The next leg follows the Waiau River as it meanders between Fiordland National Park and the Takitimu Mountains. Lake Monowai is accessed from Borland Road approximately 30 km from Manapouri. The lake is 10 km from the intersection along an easy unsealed road (NB: driving beyond Borland Lodge is not recommended as the road is narrow and poorly maintained).

Lake Hauroko – campground, picnicking, swimming, fishing
Back on the Southern Scenic Route, continue down the Waiau Valley 28 km to Clifden, site of a beautiful suspension bridge over the Waiau, opened in 1899. The 34-km side trip up the Lill Burn to Lake Hauroko begins 500 m from the bridge. The road is unsealed but in good condition; the last few kilometres to the lake is through forest. A short forest loop in the Dean Forest leads to a huge 1000-year-old totara.

Tuatapere – campground
Tuatapere, 11 km from Clifden, is the base for exploring the western reaches of the Te Wae Wae Bay coast, Rowallan Forest and multi-day tramps around Fiordland's south coast and the Hump Ridge.

Te Wae Wae Bay–Riverton – beaches, walks, swimming, campground
Ten kilometres from Tuatapere, SH 99 reaches the magnificent Te Wae Wae Bay. Between here and Riverton are several places of interest, notably McCrackens Rest (views of the bay, information on the area's natural, Maori and European history); Monkey Island, at the eastern end of the bay (sacred to Maori, site of a gold rush tent town, safe swimming, picnicking); Cosy Nook (a delightful fishing settlement); Colac Bay (excellent beach and campground). Lastly, there's Riverton's superbly located Beachfront Café (turn right at the Aparima River bridge and follow signs to Riverton Rocks), or alternatively the Thyme Out Tearooms (turn up Lex Street from the Riverton Rocks waterfront) for refreshments or a meal.

There are several scenic walks in this area – details from Riverton's information centre. The free Riverton-Aparima South Coast heritage trail brochure provides a useful history of the area.

From Riverton, allow 25 minutes to cross the Aparima and Oreti River floodplains to Invercargill.

INDEX

A bold numeral refers to a map.

Abel Tasman National Park **80**, 81, 82, **84**
Acheron House **90**
Acheron River **102**
Ahimanawa Range 68, 69
Ahipara **14**, 15
Ahuriri Flat **136**, 137
Ahuriri River **122**, 123
Aickens **110**, 113
Akaroa 106, **106**, 107
Akaroa Harbour 106, 107
Alderman Islands 31
Alex Knob 97
Alexandra **130**, 131, **132**, 133
Alford Forest **108**, 109
Amodeo Bay **28**, 29
Amuri Plain **90**, 91, 93, **94**, **102**
Amuri Range **102**, **104**, 105
Amuri Skifield **90**
Anapai Bay **80**, 82
Anaura Bay **46**, 49
Aniwaniwa **56**, 57
Aoraki/Mount Cook National Park **94**,120, 121, **122**
Aoraki/Mt Cook **94**,121, **122**
Aorangi Range 72, 74
Aorere River **80**, 83
Aotea Harbour 24
Aparima River **140**, 141
Aramoana Walkway 40
Aratiatia **32**
Aratiatia Rapids 33
Arawata River **98**, 101
Arrow River **124**, 125
Arrowtown **124**, 125
Arthur's Pass 89, 91, 95, 105, 109, **110**, 111, 112
Arthur's Pass National Park **110**, 111
Arthur's Point **124**, 125
Arundel **108**, 109
Ashburton **114**, **114**, 120
Ashburton River **114**
Athenree **28**, **44**, 45
Athol **126**, 127
Atiamuri **36**, 37
Auckland **10**, 11, **22**, 23, **24**, 25, **26**, 27, 33
Aviemore dam **118**, 119
Awakino 34, 35
Awakino Gorge 35
Awakino River **34**
Awanui **14**, **16**, **18**, 19
Awaroa **80**
Awaroa Bay 82
Awatere River **102**
Awhitu Peninsula 25

Balclutha 134, **134**, **135**, 136, **136**, 137
Banks Peninsula 106
Bannockburn 124, **124**
Barrys Bay 107
Barryville **36**
Barrytown **86**, 89
Barrytown Flats 88
Bay of Islands 11, **18**, 19, 21, **22**, 23
Bay of Plenty **32**, **44**, 45, **46**, **50**, 58
Bay View 69
Baylys Beach **10**, 12
Bealey **110**, 112
Bealey River **110**
Bealey Spur 112
Beaumont **130**, 131
Becks **132**, 133

Belgrove **84**, 85
Benmore dam 118, **118**, 119
Benneydale **36**, 37
Bethells Beach 11
Big River Track 89
Black Head 134, **134**
Blackball **86**, 89
Blackmount **140**
Blenheim **78**, 79, 85, 92, 93, **102**, 103, 105
Blue Lakes 121, **122**, 123
Blue River **98**, 101
Bluff 135, **135**
Bluff Harbour **135**
Bombay **32**, 33
Borland Rd 141
Borland Lodge **140**
Boundary Creek 101
Boundary Stream Scenic Reserve **54**, 55
Bowentown Heads **44**, 45
Boyle River **90**, 92
Bridal Veil Falls **24**, 25
Brighton 134, **134**
Broadwood **14**, 15
Broken River Skifield **110**, 112
Bruce Bay **98**, 99
Bruce Creek 112
Brynderwyn **10**, 12
Buckland Peaks 88
Buller River **84**, **86**, **90**, 91
Bulls **62**, 63, **64**, 65, **66**, 67
Burke Pass **120**, 121
Burke's Pass **120**, 121
Burster Range **94**, 97

Cable Bay **18**, 19
Cambridge **36**, 37
Cameron Flats 100
Cannibal Gorge 92
Cape Brett Peninsula **18**, 21
Cape Colville **28**, 30
Cape Egmont **60**, 61
Cape Foulwind **86**, 88
Cape Karikari **18**
Cape Kidnappers **70**, 71
Cape Maria van Diemen **16**, 17
Cape Palliser **72**, 74, 75
Cape Reinga 11, 16, **16**, 17
Cape Runaway **46**, 48
Cardrona Skifield **124**, 125
Cardrona River **124**, **130**
Carters Beach **86**, 88
Carterton **72**, 74
Cascade Creek **126**
Cascade River **98**, 101
Cass **110**, 112
Castle Hill **110**, 111
Castle Hill Scenic Reserve 111
Castlepoint **72**, 73, 74, 75
Cathedral Caves 138
Cathedral Cove 30
Catlins 114, 137
Catlins Coast 136
Catlins Coastal Rainforest Park **136**, 137
Catlins Heads 137
Catlins Lake **136**, 137
Catlins River **136**, 137
Cavalli Islands 19
Cave Stream 111, 142112
Cave Stream Scenic Reserve **110**, 111
Charleston **86**, 88
Charming Creek Walkway 87
Charwell River **102**, **104**

Chaslands **136**, 138
Cheviot **102**, 104, 105
Christchurch 83, 89, 91, 93, 95, 103, **104**, 105, 106, 106, 107, 108, 109, **110**, 111, 114, **114**, 115, 120
Clarence **102**
Clarence River **90**, 93, **102**, 103
Clarke River **98**, 100
Cleddau River **126**, 129
Clifden 140, 141
Clifton **70**, 71
Clinton 134, **135**
Clive **70**, 71
Cloudy Bay **102**
Clutha dam **130**
Clutha River 123, **130**, 131, **134**
Clyde **130**, **132**, 133
Clyde dam **132**, 133
Cobb Reservoir **80**, 82
Colac Bay **140**, 141
Collingwood **80**, 83
Colville **28**, 29
Conway River **102**, **104**, 105
Cook Flat Rd 97
Cook River **98**, 99
Cook Saddle 97
Cook Strait 75
Cooks Beach **28**, 30
Cooks Cove walkway 49
Coopers Beach **18**, 19
Copland River **98**
Copland Track 99
Coromandel **28**, 29, 30
Coromandel Forest Park 30
Coromandel Peninsula 26
Coromandel Range **28**, 30
Coronet Peak Skifield **124**, 125
Cosy Nook **140**, 141
Craigieburn Forest Park **110**, 111, 112
Craigieburn Skifield **110**, 112
Croesus Track 89
Cromwell 119, 124, **124**, 125, **130**, 131, **132**, 133
Crown Range 124, **124**, 125
Crown Terrace 125
Culverden **90**, 91, 93, **104**, 105
Curio Bay **136**, 138, 139

Dalgety Range **120**, 121, **122**
Dannevirke **70**, 71
Danseys Pass 118, 119, **132**
Darfield **110**, 111
Dargaville **10**, 13, **14**, 15, **22**, 23
Dashwood Pass 103
Davis Flat 101
Dawson Falls **60**, 61
Dean Forest 141
Deep Cove **140**, 141
Denniston **86**, 87
Denniston Plateau 87
Denniston Walkway 87
Desert Road 67
Dolomite Point **86**, 88
Domett **104**, 105
Doneraille Park **52**, 53
Donne River 129
Donnelly's Crossing **14**, 15
Doubtless Bay 11, **14**, **18**, 19
Douglas 42
Drury **24**, 25
Dune Lake 100
Dunedin 114, **116**, 117, 119, 120, **130**, 131, **132**, 133, 134, **134**

Dunstan Range **122**, 123, **124**
Duntroon **118**, 119
Duvauchelle **106**, 107
D'Urville Island **78**

East Cape **46**, 47, 48
East Egmont 63
East Woodhill Arboretum **52**
Edendale 135, **135**
Eglinton River **126**
Egmont National Park **60**, 61, **62**, 63
Egmont Village **62**, 63
Eight Mile Junction **38**, 39
Eketahuna **72**, 73
Elie de Beaumont **94**, 96
Eltham **62**, 63
Esk River 68, 69
Eskdale 68
Ettrick **130**, 131
Evans Pass 106
Eyre Mountains **126**, 127

Fairlie 109, 115, 120, **120**, 121
Fantail Bay 30
Fantail Falls **98**, 100
Farewell Spit **80**, 81, 83
Featherston **72**, 73, 74
Ferry Landing 30
Fiordland National Park **126**, 127, **140**, 141
Firth of Thames **24**, 27, **28**
Five Rivers **126**, 127
Flaxmill Bay 30
Fletcher Bay **28**, 30
Flock Hill **110**, 111, 112
Florence Hill 138
Forest Tower Walk 37
Fortrose 136, 138, 139
Fossil Point 83
Foveaux Strait 139
Fox Glacier (village) **94**, 97, **98**, 99
Fox Glacier **94**, 97
Fox River **86**, 88
Foxton **64**, 65
Foxton Beach **64**
Franz Josef **94**, 95, 96, 97, **98**
Franz Josef Glacier **94**, 96
Frasertown **52**, 53
French Hill 107
French Pass **78**, 79

Gabriel's Gully **130**, 131
Gates of Haast **98**, 100
Gebbies Pass 106, **106**, 107
Geraldine **108**, 109, 115, 120, **120**, 121
Gertrude Valley 129
Gillespies Beach **94**, 97
Gisborne **46**, 47, 48, 49, **50**, 51, **52**, 53
Glentunnel **108**, 109
Gloriana Peak **90**, 92
Goat Island Marine Reserve **22**, 23
Golden Bay **80**, 81, 82, 83, **84**
Golden Downs Forest **84**, 85
Golden Springs **32**, 33
Gore 131, 134, 135, **134**, **135**
Gore Bay **104**, 105
Gowanbridge **84**, 85
Granity **86**, 87
Green Island 134, **134**
Greenstone track 128
Grey River **86**
Greymouth **86**, 88, 89, **94**, 95, **110**, 111, 113

Greytown 72, 73, 74
Grove Arm 79
Gunn's Camp 126, 129

Haast 98, 100, 101
Haast Pass 91, 98, 99, 100
Haast River 98, 100
Hahei 28, 30
Haldane 136, 139
Haldane Bay 136, 139
Hamilton 24, 25, 28, 32, 33, 34, 35, 36, 37, 39
Hampden 116, 117
Hangaroa River 52, 53
Hanging Rock 121
Hanmer Forest 93
Hanmer Springs 90, 91, 93, 102, 104, 105
Hannah's Clearing 98, 101
Hapuka Estuary 98, 101
Harihari 94, 96
Harihari Coastal Walk 96
Harrison Scenic Reserve 20
Haruru Falls 20
Harwood Hole 80, 82
Hastings 70, 71
Hatfields Beach 22, 23
Hauhangaroa Range 36
Haumoana 70, 71
Hauraki Gulf 24, 26, 28, 29
Haurangi Forest Park 72, 75
Havelock 78, 79
Hawea 98, 101
Hawera 60, 60, 61, 62, 63
Hawkdun Range 132, 133
Hawke Bay 52, 54, 55, 56, 68
Hawke's Lookout 82
Heaphy Track 83, 87
Helena Bay 18, 21
Helensville 10, 12
Herekawa Scenic Reserve 37
Herekino 14, 15
Hicks Bay 46, 48
Hikuai 28, 31
Himatangi Beach 64, 65
Hokianga Harbour 14, 15, 22, 23
Hokitika 94, 95
Hollyford Rd 128
Hollyford River 126, 128, 129
Homer Saddle 129
Homer Tunnel 126, 129
Hook 115, 116
Hooker Range 98, 100
Hooker/Landsborough Wilderness Area 99, 100
Hope Saddle 84, 85
Hot Water Beach 28, 30
Hoteo North 10, 12
Houhora 16, 17
Houhora Harbour 16, 17
Huiarau Range 50, 51, 56, 57
Huka Falls 32, 33
Humboldt Mountains 126, 128
Hump Ridge 140, 141
Hundalee 104
Hunua Range 26, 27
Hurunui 90, 93
Hurunui River 90, 93

Ikamatua 86, 89
Inangahua 85, 89
Inangahua Junction 84, 86, 89, 90
Inglewood 62, 63
Inland Kaikoura Range 102, 103

Invercargill 134, 135, 135, 136, 136, 137, 138, 139, 140, 141
Iwikau Village 38, 39

Jackson Bay 98, 100, 101
Jacksons 86, 89, 110, 113
Jacksons Rd 79
Jacobs River 98, 99
Jerusalem 38, 41
Jollies Pass 90, 93

Kaeo 18, 19
Kahurangi National Park 79, 80, 82, 83, 84, 86, 87
Kaiaua 26, 27
Kaikohe 14, 15, 22, 23
Kaikoura 93, 102, 103, 104, 105
Kaikoura Mountains 102, 104
Kaikoura Peninsula 102, 104
Kaingaroa Forest 32, 33, 56, 57
Kaipara Harbour 10, 11
Kaipara River 12
Kaitaia 14, 15, 16, 16, 18, 19, 22, 23
Kaiteriteri 80
Kaka Point 136, 137
Kakapotahi Scenic Reserve 94, 95
Kakatahi 38, 41
Kapiti Coast 65
Kapiti Island 64, 73
Kaponga 60, 61
Karaka Bay 46
Karamea 86, 87
Karamea Bluff Ecological Reserve 87
Karangahake 28
Karangahake Gorge 28, 31
Karangahake Gorge Historic Walkway 31
Karangarua River 98, 99
Karekare 10
Karekare Beach 11
Karikari Peninsula 18, 19
Karioi 35
Karitane 116, 117
Katikati 44, 45
Katiki 116
Katiki Beach 117
Kauaeranga 28
Kauaeranga River 28
Kauri Grove 30
Kawakawa 18, 20, 22
Kawakawa Bay 26, 27
Kawarau Gorge 124, 125
Kawarau River 124, 125, 126, 130
Kawatiri Junction 84, 85
Kawerau 58, 59
Kawhia 24, 25, 34, 35
Kawhia Harbour 24, 34, 35
Kekerengu 102, 103
Kenepuru Sound 78, 79
Kennedy Bay 28
Kereta 28, 29
Kerikeri 18, 20
Kerikeri River 18
Key Summit 126, 128
Kilmog Hill 117
Kingston 126, 127
Kinleith 32, 33
Kinleith Forest 32, 33, 36, 37
Klondyke Corner 112
Knights Point 98, 99
Knobby Range 130, 131
Knobs Flat 126, 128
Kohaihai 86, 87
Kohatu Junction 80, 84, 85

Kohukohu 14, 15
Koriniti 38, 41
Kuaotunu 28, 30
Kumara 110
Kumara Junction 110, 113
Kumeu 10, 11
Kuratau Junction 36, 37, 38, 41
Kurow 115, 118, 119
Kyeburn 132, 133

Lake Aviemore 118, 118, 119
Lake Benmore 118, 119
Lake Brunner 86, 89, 110, 113
Lake Coleridge 110
Lake Dunstan 124, 124, 130, 131, 132, 133
Lake Ellesmere 106, 107
Lake Ferry 72, 75
Lake Forsyth 106, 107
Lake Gunn 126, 128
Lake Hauroko 140, 141
Lake Hawea 98, 101, 122, 124
Lake Ianthe 94, 95, 96
Lake Kaniere 94, 95, 110
Lake Karapiro 36, 37
Lake Lyndon 110, 111
Lake Mahinapua 94, 95
Lake Manapouri 140, 141
Lake Mapourika 94, 96
Lake Maraetai 36, 37
Lake Marian 126, 128
Lake Matheson 94, 97
Lake Moeraki 98, 99
Lake Monowai 140, 141
Lake Ohau 122, 123
Lake Okareka 58, 59
Lake Okataina 58, 59
Lake Paringa 98, 99
Lake Pearson 110, 112
Lake Pukaki 120, 121, 122
Lake Rotoehu 58, 59
Lake Rotoiti (North Island) 58, 59
Lake Rotoiti (South Island) 84, 90
Lake Rotokakahi 58, 59
Lake Rotoma 58, 59
Lake Rotopounamu 66, 67
Lake Rotoroa 84, 85, 90
Lake Rotorua 32, 33, 56, 58, 59
Lake Roxburgh 131
Lake Ruataniwha 122, 123
Lake Tarawera 58, 59
Lake Taupo 32, 33, 36, 37, 38, 41, 66, 67, 68
Lake Te Anau 126, 127, 128, 140
Lake Tekapo 120, 121, 122
Lake Tennyson 90, 93
Lake Tikitapu 58, 59
Lake Tutira 54, 55
Lake Tutira Reserve 55
Lake Wahapo 94, 96
Lake Waihola 134, 134
Lake Waikaremoana 56, 57
Lake Wairarapa 72
Lake Waitaki 118, 118, 119
Lake Wakatipu 124, 125, 126, 127, 130
Lake Wanaka 98, 99, 100, 101, 122, 123, 124, 124, 125
Lake Whakamaru 36
Lake Wilkie 138
Lake Wombat 96
Lake Benmore 118
Landsborough River 98, 100
Langs Beach 22, 23

Lauder 133
Lawrence 130, 131
Le Bons Bay 106, 107
Leigh 22, 23
Levin 64, 73
Lewis Pass 90, 91, 92, 105
Lewis Pass National Reserve 91
Lewis River 90
Ligar Bay 80, 82
Lill Burn 140, 141
Lindis Pass 120, 122, 123
Lindis Pass Scenic Reserve 123
Lindis River 122, 123
Linkwater 78, 79
Little Akaloa Bay 106, 107
Little River 106, 107
Little Wanganui 86, 87
Long Bay 29
Long Bay Rd 107
Lower Buller Gorge 85
Lower Moutere 80, 81
Lower Waitaki 119
Lyell 84, 85
Lynmore 58, 59
Lyttelton Harbour 106, 106

Macetown 124, 125
Mackay Creek 126, 128
Mackenzie Basin 120, 121, 123
Maclennan 136, 137
Maclennan Range 136, 138
Mahia 52, 53
Mahia Beach 52, 53
Mahia Peninsula 52, 53, 54
Mahinapua Walkway 95
Mahitahi River 98, 99
Main Divide 112
Makarora 98, 100, 101
Makarora River 98
Makomako 24, 25
Mamaku Plateau 32, 33
Manaia (Coromandel) 28, 29
Manaia (Taranaki) 60, 61
Manapouri 140, 141
Manapouri Power Station 140
Manawatu Gorge Scenic Reserve 70, 71
Manawatu River 65, 70, 72
Mandeville 135, 135
Mangakino 36, 37
Mangamuka 22
Mangamuka Bridge 14, 15, 22, 23
Mangamuka Gorge Scenic Reserve 22, 23
Manganui Skifield 62, 63
Manganuku 50, 51
Mangapai River 22, 23
Mangataínoka 72, 73
Mangatainoka River 73
Mangatarata 32, 33
Mangawhai 22, 23
Mangawhai Harbour 22
Mangawhai Heads 22, 23
Mangawhero River 38, 41
Mangonui 18, 19
Mangonui Harbour 18
Maniototo Plain 132, 133
Manuherikia River 130, 132, 133
Manukau Harbour 10, 24, 25, 26
Mapua 80, 81
Marahau 80, 81
Marble Hill 91
Marble Hill Scenic Reserve 91
Maerewhenua River 118, 119, 132
Marian Creek 128

Marlborough 79, 103
Marokopa 34, 35
Marokopa Falls 34, 35
Marsden Point 22, 23
Martinborough 72, 73, 74
Marton 66
Martyr Saddle 98, 101
Maruia 90
Maruia Falls 90, 91
Maruia River 90, 91, 92
Maruia Springs 90, 91, 92
Masterton 72, 73, 75
Matakana Island 44, 45
Matakohe 10, 12
Matamata 32, 33
Matata 44, 45
Mataura 135, **135**
Mataura River 135, **135**
Matauri Bay 18, 19
Matawai 50, 51
Matawhero 53
Matingarahi 26, 27
Matukituki River 122, 123
Maungaharuru Range 68, 69
Mavora Lakes 126, 127
Mavora Lakes Park 127
McCrackens Rest 141
Meeting of the Waters Scenic Reserve 63
Mercury Bay 28, 30
Mercury Islands 28
Methven 108, 109, 114, 114
Middlemarch 119, **132**, 133
Middleton Bay 61
Milford Sound 91, **126**, 127, 128, 129
Milford Track 128
Millers Flat 130, 131
Millerton 87
Milton 130, **131**
Minginui 56, 57
Miranda 26, 27
Mirror Lakes 126, 128
Mitre Peak 126, 129
Moana 110, 113
Moehau Range 28, 30
Moeraki 116, 117
Moeraki Beach 116, 117
Moeraki Boulders 117
Mohaka River 68, 69
Mohuiti 14, 15
Mokau 34, 35
Mokihinui 86, 87
Mokihinui River 86
Molesworth Road 102, 105
Molesworth Station 93
Molyneux Bay 136, 137
Monkey Island 140, 141
Monro Beach 98, 99
Morere 52, 53
Mosgiel 132, 133
Mosquito Bay 12
Mossburn 126, 127
Motu 50
Motu River 50, 51
Motueka 80, 81, 82, 83, **84**, 85
Motueka River 80, 83, **84**
Motupiko 84, 85
Mount Aspiring National Park 98, 100, 101, 120, **122**, 123, 128
Mount Bruce 72, 73, 74
Mount Cook Village 109, 114, 115, 121, **122**
Mount Maunganui 44, 45
Moutere Inlet 81

Mt Arthur 80, 83, **84**
Mt Arthur Range 80, 81, **84**
Mt Aspiring 123
Mt Barrier 126, 129
Mt Bealey 110
Mt Bruce 73
Mt Bruce National Wildlife Centre 73
Mt Cheeseman Skifield 110, 111
Mt Cook – see Aoraki/Mt Cook
Mt Crosscut 126, 128
Mt Egmont – see Mt Taranaki
Mt Haast 86, 89
Mt Hikurangi 46, 48
Mt Hooker 98, 100
Mt Hutt 108, 109
Mt Hutt Skifield 109, 114
Mt Iron 122, 123
Mt Karioi 24, 25, **34**
Mt Lyford 105
Mt Lyford Skifield 104, 105
Mt Messenger 34, 35
Mt One One 94, 96
Mt Owen 85, 86
Mt Ngauruhoe 38, 66
Mt Pirongia 35, **34**
Mt Rolleston 110, 112
Mt Roy 122, 123
Mt Ruapehu 38, 66
Mt Rutland 90, 91
Mt Talbot 126, 129
Mt Tapuae-o-Uenuku 102, 103, 105
Mt Taranaki 60, 61, **62**, 63
Mt Tongariro 38, 39, 66
Mt Tutoko 126, 129
Mt Pirongia 34, 35
Murchison 84, 85, **86**, 90, 91, 92
Murchison Mountains 126, 127, 128, **140**
Muriwai 11
Muriwai Beach 10, 11
Murray Creek 89
Murupara 56, 57

Napier 52, 53, 54, 55, 68, 69, **70**, 71
Naseby 119, **132**, 133
National Park 38, 39, 67
Neils Beach 98, 101
Nelson 78, 79, 80, 81, 84, 85
Nelson Lakes National Park 84, 85, **90**
Nevins Lookout 43
Nevis River 124, 125, **130**
New Plymouth 34, 35, 37, 39, 60, 60, **62**, 63
Ngaiotonga 18, 21
Ngakawau 86, 87
Ngaruawahia 24, 25
Ngatapa 52, 53
Ngatimoti 80, 83
Ngawi 72, 75
Ngongotaha 32, 33
Nile River 86, 88
Ninety Mile Beach 14, 15, **16**, 17
Norsewood 70, 71
North Cape 16, 17
North Egmont
North Rough Ridge 133
Nugget Point 136, 137
Nuhaka 52, 53

Oakleigh 22, 23
Oakura 60, 60
Oamaru 115, **116**, 117, 118, **118**, 119, 121, 123
Oaonui 60, 61
Oaro 104, 105

Ocean Beach (Coromandel) 31
Ocean Beach (Kawhai) 35
Ocean Beach (Hawke's Bay) **70**, 71
Ohaeawai 22, 23
Ohakea 62
Ohakune 38, 40, **66**, 67
Ohau Point 102, 103
Ohau Skifield 122, 123
Ohinemuri River 31
Ohiwa 44
Ohiwa Harbour 44, 45
Ohope 44, 45
Okains Bay 106, 107
Okarito 94, 96
Okarito Forest 94, 96
Okarito Lagoon 94, 96
Okato 60, 60
Okiore 50
Okiwi Bay 78, 79
Okuru 98, 101
Old Man Range 130, 131
Omahuta Forests 22, 23
Omanu Beach 44, 45
Omapere 14, 15
Omarama 115, 118, **118**, 121, **122**, 123
Omeru Reserve 12
Omori 38, 41
Onaero 34, 35
Onaero Beach 35
Onekaka 80, 83
Onemana 28, 31
Onepoto 56, 57
Ongaonga 70, 71
Oparara 86, 87
Oparara limestone arches 86, 87
Oparau 34, 35
Opihi River 120, 121
Opononi 14, 15
Opotiki 44, 45, **46**, 47, **50**, 51, 53
Opouri Saddle 79
Opoutama 52, 53
Opoutere 28, 31
Opua 18, 20, 21
Opuha River 120, 121
Opunake 60, 61
Oraka Beach 52, 53
Orere 26, 27
Orere Point 26, 27
Orete Point 46, 47
Oreti River 140, 141
Orewa 22, 23
Ormond 50, 51
Orokawa Bay 44, 45
Oruaiti Beach 46, 47
Otago Peninsula 116, 130, **132**
Otaio 115, **116**
Otaio Beach 115
Otaki 64, 65
Otara 136, 139
Otatara 136, 137
Otematata 118, 119
Otiki Hill 48
Otira 110, 113
Otira Gorge 110
Otira River 110, 111, 113
Otoko 50, 51
Otorohanga 25, **34**, 35
Oue 14, 15
Outram 132, 133
Owaka 136, 137
Oxford 105, **108**, 109

Paekakariki 64, 65
Paeroa 28

Pahiatua 72, 73
Paihia 18, 20
Pakawau 80, 83
Pakiroa Beach 88
Palliser Bay 72, 73, 74, 75
Palmerston 116, 117, **132**, 133
Palmerston North 70, 71, **72**, 73
Papaaroha 28, 29
Papakura 26, 27
Papamoa Beach 44, 45
Paparata Saddle 42, 43
Paparoa National Park 86, 88
Paparoa Range 86, 89
Papatea Bay 46
Papatowai 136, 138
Papiiora Ridge 57
Parakai 10, 12
Parapara Inlet 80, 83
Paraparaumu 64, 65
Parekura Bay 18, 21
Parengarenga Harbour 16, **16**, 17
Parihaka 61
Paringa 98, 99
Paringa River 98, 99
Patea 62, 65
Paturau River 80, 83
Patutahi 52
Pauanui 28, 30
Pauanui Mountain 31
Paynes Ford Scenic Reserve 80, 82
Peel Forest 108, 109
Pelorus Bridge 78, 79
Pelorus River 78, 79, 80
Pelorus Sound 78, 79
Peters Pool 96
Piako-Waihou Basin 33
Picnic Point 138
Picton 78, 79, 93, 102, 103, 109
Pigeon Bay 106, 107
Piha 10, 11
Pinnacles 31
Piopio 34, 35
Pipiriki 38, 40
Pirongia 34, 35
Pleasant Flat 98, 100
Pleasant Point 120, 121
Poerua River 94, 96
Pohara 80
Pohara Beach 82
Pohokura 42, 43
Pohokura Saddle 42, 43
Ponui Island 26, 27
Porangahau 70, 71
Porpoise Bay 136, 138
Port Albert 10, 12
Port Hills 106, **106**
Port Jackson 28, 30
Port Levy 106, 107
Port Underwood 102
Portage 78, 79
Porter Heights Skifield 110, 111
Porters Pass 110, 111
Pouawa 46, 48, 49
Pounawea 136, 137
Poverty Bay 50, 51, **52**, 53
Pukekohe 24, 25
Pukekura 94, 95
Puketi Forest 18, 19, **22**
Puketona 18, 20
Punakaiki 86, 88
Pungarehu 60, 60, 61
Puniho 60, **60**
Puponga 80, 83

Pupu Walkway **80**, 82
Purakaunui Bay **136**, 137
Purakaunui Falls **136**, 137
Pureora 36, 37
Pureora Forest Park 36, 37, **38**
Purple Hill 112
Putangirua Pinnacles **72**, 75
Putararu 32, 33

Queen Charlotte Drive **78**, 79
Queen Charlotte Sound **78**, 79
Queenstown 118, 124, **124**, 125, **126**, 127, **130**, 131

Rabbit Island **80**, 81
Radiant Range **86**, 87
Raes Junction **130**, 131
Raetihi 38, 40
Ragged Ridge 133
Raglan 24, 25, **34**, 35
Raglan Harbour 24, 25
Rahu Saddle **86**, 89, 91
Rai Valley **78**, 79
Raio 16, 17
Rakaia **114**, 120
Rakaia Gorge **108**, 109
Raikaia River **108**, **110**, 114
Ranfurly 119, **132**, 133
Rangiora 106, **108**, 109, **110**
Rangipo 66
Rangipo Desert **66**, 67
Rangitaiki River **58**, 59
Rangitata **108**, **114**, 115, 120, **120**
Rangitata River **108**, 109, **114**, **120**
Rangatikei River **64**, 65
Rapaura Rd **78**, 79
Raukumara Range 46, 47, 48, **50**, 51
Raurimu **38**, 39
Raurimu Spiral 39
Rawene **14**, 15
Rawhiti **18**, 21
Red Hills 101
Red Tussock Conservation Area 127
Reefton **86**, 89
Reefton Saddle 89
Renwick 78
Richmond **80**, 81, **84**, 85
Rimutaka Range **72**, 74
Ripponvale 124, **124**
Riverton **140**, 141
Riwaka **80**, 81
Riwaka River **80**, 82
Roaring Bay 137
Rock and Pillar Range **130**, **132**, 133
Ross 94, 95
Ross Historic Goldfields 95
Rotorua 32, 33, **56**, 57, 58, 59
Routeburn Track 128
Rowallan Forest **140**, 141
Roxburgh **130**, 131
Roxburgh Hydro Village **130**, 131
Ruahine Range 70, 71, **72**
Ruakituri River **52**
Ruamahanga River **72**, 74
Ruatahuna **56**, 57
Ruataniwha Inlet **80**, 83
Ruato **58**, 59
Ruatoria 46, 48
Ruby Bay **80**, 81
Ruffe Creek 91
Russell **18**, 20, 21

Sanson 62, **64**, 65

Scotsmans Point 71
Scotts Beach 87
Seacliff **116**
Seal Island 88
Sealy Tarns 121
Seaward Kaikoura Range **102**, 103, 105
Seddon **102**, 103
Sentinel Rock 96
Shag Point **116**, 117
Shag River **116**, 117
Shakespear Regional Park 23
Shakespeare Cliff 30
Shannon 73
Shantytown **94**, 95
Shelly Bay 29
Shelly Beach **10**, 12
Shenandoah River **90**, 91
Shenandoah Saddle 91
Ship Creek **98**, 99
Sinclair Wetlands 134
Slope Point **136**, 139
Smoothwater Bay 101
South Fiord **126**, 128
South Head **10**
South Head Peninsula **10**, 12
South Taranaki Bight 61
Southern Alps **90**, 91, 95, 96, 97, 100, 110, 111, 120, 121, **122**, 128
Spenser Mountains **90**
Spirits Bay **16**, 17
Spooners Range 85
Spring Creek **78**, 79
Springfield **108**, **110**, 111, 113
Springs Junction **86**, 89, **90**, 91
St Albans 25
St Arnaud **84**, 85
St Bathans **132**, 133
St James Walkway 92
Stavely **108**, 109
Stewart Island 139
Stillwater **86**, 89
Stratford 42, 43, **62**, 63
Stuart Mountains **126**, 128
Summit Road 106
Sumner 106, **106**
Surat Bay **136**, 137

Taffytown Hill 87
Tahakopa Bay **136**, 137
Tahakopa River 137
Tahora 42
Tahora Saddle 42, 43
Tai Poutini/Westland National Park **94**, 95, 96, 97, **98**
Taieri Mouth 134, **134**
Taieri Plains 134
Taieri River **132**, 133, 134, **134**
Taihape **66**, 67
Taipa **18**, 19
Tairua 28, 30, 31
Tairua Harbour 28, 30
Takaka **80**, 82, 83
Takaka Hill 81, 82
Takaka Hill Walkway 82
Takaka River 82
Takapau 71, 73
Takau Bay 18
Takiora rock drawings **118**, 119
Takitimu Mountains **140**, 141
Tane Mahuta 11
Tangarakau Gorge 42
Tangarakau Gorge Scenic Reserve 43
Tangarakau River 42

Tangoio **54**, 55
Tangoio Falls Scenic Reserve **54**, 55
Tapapa 32, 33
Tapawera **80**, 83
Tapotupotu Bay **16**, 17
Tapu 28, 29
Tarakohe 82
Taramakau River **110**, 113
Tararua Range 70, 71, 72, 73, 74
Tarawera **68**, 69
Tarras **122**, 123
Tasman **80**, 81
Tasman Bay 78, 79, **80**, 82
Tasman Glacier 121, 123
Tasman River 121, **122**
Taumarunui 38, 39, 40, **42**, 43
Taupeupe Saddle **56**, 57
Taupo 32, 33, **36**, 37, **38**, 65, **66**, 67, **68**, 69
Tauranga 44, 45
Tauranga Bay (North Island) **18**, 19,
Tauranga Bay (South Island) **86**, 88
Tauranga Harbour 44, 45
Tauranga Track 51
Tautuku Bay **136**, 138
Tautuku Beach 138
Tautuku Peninsula 138
Tautuku Scenic Reserve 138
Te Ana Falls 55
Te Anau **126**, 127, 128, **140**, 141
Te Anau Downs **126**, 128
Te Anga 34, 35
Te Araroa 46, 48
Te Awamutu **34**, 35
Te Henga **10**, 11
Te Humenga Pt **72**, 75
Te Kaha 46, 47
Te Karaka **50**, 51
Te Kauwhata 24, 25
Te Kopi 75
Te Kuiti 34, 35, 36, 37, **38**, 39
Te Mata 24, 25
Te Mata Peak 70, 71
Te Morehu Scenic Reserve 27
Te Ngae **58**, 59
Te Paki **16**, 17
Te Puia 48, 49
Te Puia Springs 46, 49
Te Puke 44, 45, **58**, 59
Te Reinga **52**, 53
Te Reinga Falls 53
Te Tapuwae O Rongokako Marine Reserve 49
Te Urewera National Park **52**, 53, **54**, 56, 57
Te Urewera Range 57
Te Wae Wae Bay **140**, 141
Te Wahipounamu South-West New Zealand World Heritage Area **94**, 95, **98**, 99, 120, 127
Te Waikoropupu (Pupu) Springs 82
Te Wairoa **58**, 59
Te Werahi Beach **16**, 17
Te Whanganui-A-Hei Marine Reserve 30
Tekapo 120, 121, **122**
Tekapo Canal **122**, 121
Temple Basin Skifield **110**, 112
Temuka 114
Tengawai River **120**, 121
Tennyson Inlet **78**, 79
Thames 26, 27, **28**, 29, 31
The Chasm **126**, 129
The Divide **126**, 128

The Key **126**, 127
The Remarkables **124**, 125, **126**, 130
Thunder Creek Falls **98**, 100
Tikitere (Hells Gate Thermal Reserve) **58**, 59
Tikitiki 46, 47, 48
Timaru 114, 115, **116**, 120
Tiniroto **52**, 53
Tirau 32, 33, **36**, 37
Titirangi 10, 11
Tohunga Junction **38**, 40
Tokaanu **38**, 41
Tokata Flats 48
Tokatea Lookout 29
Tokerau Beach **18**, 19
Toko **42**, 43
Tokomaru Bay 46, 49
Tokoroa 32, 33, **36**, 37
Tolaga Bay 46, 47, 49
Tongaporutu 34, 35
Tongariro National Park **38**, 39, 65, **66**
Torlesse Gap 111
Torlesse Range **110**, 111
Totara Avenue **80**, 83
Totara North **18**, 19
Totara Walk 37
Totaranui **80**, 82
Trouson Kauri Park **14**, 15
Trumans Track 88
Tuai **56**, 57
Tuamarina **102**, 103
Tuatapere **140**, 141
Tuai **54**, 55
Turangi **36**, 37, **38**, 39, **66**, 67
Turoa Skifield **38**, 40
Tutira **54**, 55
Tutoko River **126**, 129
Twizel **122**, 123
Two Thumb Range **120**, 121

Upokongaro **38**, 41
Upper Moutere **80**, 81
Upper Takaka **80**, 82
Urenui 34, 35

Victoria Forest Park 89
Victoria Range **86**, 89, **90**, 91
Victoria Valley 22, 23
Virginia Lake 65

Waddington 105, **108**, 109
Waiapu Mountains 48
Waiapu River 46, 48
Waiau (North Island) 28
Waiau 90, **102**, 105
Waiau Falls 30
Waiau River **90**, 91, 93
Waiau River **140**, 141
Waihaha Scenic Reserve 41
Waihau Bay 46, 47
Waiheke Island 26, 27
Waihi 28, 31, **44**, 45
Waihi Beach 28, 44, 45
Waiho River **94**, 96
Waihola 134
Waihuka River **50**, 51
Waikanae **64**, 65
Waikato River 24, **32**, 33, 36, 37
Waikawa **136**, 138
Waikino 28, 31
Waikouaiti **116**, 117
Waikukupa Forest **94**, 97
Waima 46, 49
Waimakariri River **110**, 112

Waimamaku **14**, 15
Waimangaroa **86**, 87
Waimangu **32**, 33
Waimarama **70**, 71
Waimate 115, **116**, **118**
Waimauku **10**, 11
Waimea Estuary **80**, 81
Waimea Plains 81
Waimea River **80**
Waingaro **24**, 25
Wainui Bay **80**, 82
Waioeka Gorge 51
Waioeka Pa **50**
Waioeka River **50**, 51
Waiohine River **72**, 74
Waiotapu **32**, 33
Waiototo **98**, 101
Waiouru **66**, 67
Waipa Basin 35
Waipa River **34**
Waipahihi Botanical Reserve 33
Waipaoa River **52**, 53
Waipapa Bay **102**, 103
Waipara **90**, 91, 93, **104**, 105
Waipati Beach **136**, 138
Waipawa **70**, 71
Waipiro Bay **46**
Waipoua Forest **14**, 15
Waipu **22**, 23
Waipu Cove **22**, 23
Waipukarau **70**, 71
Waipunga Falls **68**, 69
Waipunga River **68**
Wairakei **32**, 33
Wairata **50**
Wairau River **102**, 103
Wairoa **52**, 53, **54**, 55, **56**, 57
Waitaha River **94**, 95
Waitaha Scenic Reserve **94**, 95
Waitakere **10**
Waitakere Range **10**, 11
Waitaki Dam 119
Waitaki River 115, **116**, 118, **118**, 119
Waitaki Valley 114, 123
Waitangi **18**, 20
Waitangiroto Lagoon **94**, 96
Waitangiroto River **94**
Waitara **34**
Waitara River **34**
Waitati **116**, 117
Waitiki Landing 16, **16**, 17
Waitomo Caves **34**, 35
Waituhi Lookout 41
Waituhi Saddle **38**
Waiuku **24**, 25
Waiuta 89
Waiuta mine **86**
Waiwera **22**, 23
Wakefield **84**
Waldronville 134, **134**
Wanaka **98**, 99, 101, 118, 120, **122**, 123, 124, **124**, 125, **130**, 131
Wanganui **38**, 39, 40, **62**, 63, 65, **66**, 67
Wanganui River **94**, 96
Wangapeka Track 83
Ward **102**, 103
Warea 60, **60**
Warkworth **22**, 23
Warrington **116**, 117
Washdyke **108**, 109, **114**, 115, 120, **120**, 121
Waterfall Track 92
Waverley **62**, 65

Weka Pass 105
Wellington **64**, 65, **72**, 73, 74
Wellsford **10**, 12
Westport **84**, 85, **86**, 87, 88, 89, 91
Whakaki Lagoon **52**, 53, **54**
Whakamaru **36**, 37
Whakapapa **38**, 39, **66**, 67
Whakapara **18**, 21, **22**
Whakapohai Wildlife Refuge 99
Whakarewarewa **32**, 33
Whakarewarewa Forest Park 59
Whakatane **44**, 45, **58**, 59
Whakatane River **58**
Whales Back Saddle **104**, 105
Whanarua Bay **46**, 47
Whangaimoana **72**, 75
Whangamata **28**, 31
Whangamomona **42**, 43
Whangamomona Saddle **42**, 43
Whanganui Inlet **80**, 83
Whanganui National Park **38**, 39, 40
Whanganui River **38**, 39, 40, **62**, 65
Whangaparaoa **46**, 47, 48
Whangaparaoa Peninsula **22**, 23
Whangapoua Harbour **28**, 30
Whangarei **10**, **18**, 20, **22**, 23
Whangarei Harbour **22**, 23
Whangaroa **18**, 19
Whangaroa Harbour 19
Whangaruru **18**
Whangaruru Harbour **18**, 21
Whangaruru North **18**
Whangaruru North Head 21
Wharariki Beach **80**, 83
Wharekai Te Kau wildlife refuge 101
Wharekawa Harbour **28**, 31
Wharerata Forest **52**, 53
Whataroa **94**, 95, 96
Whatawhata **34**, 35
Whenuakite **28**, 30
Whirinaki Forest Park **56**, 57
Whiritoa **28**
Whiritoa Beach 31
White Cliffs Walkway 35
White Island 47
White Pine Bush Reserve 55
Whitianga **28**, 30
Willsher Bay **136**, 137
Winchester **108**, 109
Windwhistle **108**, 109
Woodend **104**, 105, **106**, **108**, 109, 115, 120
Woodpecker Bay **86**, 88
Woodville **70**, 71, **72**, 73